CHRIST IN ME

A Study of the Mind of Christ in Paul

DERRICK GREEVES

LONDON

THE EPWORTH PRESS

FIRST PUBLISHED IN 1962

© THE EPWORTH PRESS 1962

Book Steward
FRANK H. CUMBERS

SET IN MONOTYPE IMPRINT AND PRINTED IN
GREAT BRITAIN BY THE CAMELOT PRESS LTD
LONDON AND SOUTHAMPTON

Contents

PREFACE	vii
INTRODUCTION	1
1 MY GOSPEL	5
2 MY MIND	18
3 MY FACE IN THE FLESH	27
4 MY GOD	34
5 MY SAVIOUR	42
6 MY KINSMEN	54
7 MY BELOVED IN THE LORD	67
8 MY MINISTRY	78
9 MY SUFFERINGS	90
10 MY MANNER OF LIFE	99
11 MY NEIGHBOUR	108
12 MY BODY	125
ADDITIONAL NOTE	137

Preface

THESE CHAPTERS are offered to anyone who will spend a few hours with the New Testament in order to reaffirm the fact that we have no Saviour but Jesus and that Paul is truly one of His prophets.

My interest in this theme began as a schoolboy on Saturday afternoon walks with my father on the slopes of the Pennines. My only regret is that he is not still alive to correct errors of fact and judgement.

Apart from acknowledging my debt to him, I cannot attempt to assess what other teachers have given. It is often as hard to trace the source of the thoughts in one's mind as it is to identify the origin of the cells in one's body.

I have quoted extensively from the New Testament, but I am fully aware of the danger of extracting a text from its context. I have tried scrupulously to quote Paul only when I have felt sure that the passage quoted was not merely an isolated idea, but in harmony with his doctrine as a whole.

The reader will not need to be reminded that the gospels as we know them did not exist when Paul wrote his epistles. We must constantly beware of thinking of St Paul as having read the gospels and then having decided to revise their message.

One further point: I have made use of all the Epistles from Romans to Philemon as being Pauline. There seems little doubt that other writers had a hand in the compiling of Ephesians and the Pastorals as we now have them. But I take the admittedly conservative view that their originator was Paul himself. As with many other New Testament problems, I hope one day to hear a full account from the writers concerned!

WESTMINSTER
January 1962

Introduction

EVERY CHRISTIAN needs to be reminded time and again concerning the unity of the Faith. We do not worship three Gods, but one. We do not hold two Bibles in our hand, but one. Nor do we proclaim two Gospels, but one.

There is a misunderstanding which has recurred through the centuries: that there are two Christianities, that of Jesus and that of Paul. The scholar in some erudite publication attempts to prove that Paul has perverted the Gospel of Christ and has caused us to sit more at the feet of his teacher, Gamaliel, than at the feet of the Galilean Master. The Christian beginner reads the Epistles of Paul and lays them down despairingly with the cry: 'Why must we have all this tangle of theology? Why cannot we keep to the simple teaching of Christ? Give me the Sermon on the Mount, and the Cross of Calvary and the Empty Tomb, and I have all that is needed to make a Christian. Why all this involved panegyric about Christ at the beginning of Ephesians, or this technical discussion about Christian ethics in Corinthians, or this complicated argument in Galatians?' (Blessed be the *New English Bible* for its unravelling!)

This sounds plausible enough, but like many plausible ideas, it is both inadequate and inaccurate. Men may imagine themselves to be so clear of vision that they need no interpreters. God thought otherwise; in His inscrutable wisdom He saw fit to inspire men to expound even the Word made flesh. Alongside the Gospels, the Acts of the Apostles and the Epistles are all part of the revelation of His unsearchable riches.

So the main purpose of this book is to show that, far from perverting the Gospel, St Paul has elucidated and adorned it. He did not exaggerate when he claimed to have the mind of Christ. Paul was a Christian *par excellence*. He let Christ come alive in him. It was not that he merely became a passive agent of Christ, as though he were a spiritualistic medium of a dead 'control'. It was the case of a new creation from within. It was Paul who was dead, and Christ who was alive. If Paul were to ask us, 'Who do men say that I am?' we might answer: 'It is no longer Saul of Tarsus, but Paul in whom dwells the living water of eternal Life.' He is a new creature; his very selfhood has been replaced by the love and mind and will of Christ.

Paul had taken Christ so much as his Master that his whole being was at Christ's beck and call. They used to say of a slave that he was his master's 'other self'. He was his master's representative, memory, tool, his very hands and feet. And this was Paul's proud role. Christ wants each of us to be his *alter ego*, and Paul was the first to know what it means to say 'I am no longer my own, but Christ's'. He even dared to say: 'It is no longer I, but Christ.'

I believe it is true to say that just as in Christ we find as much of the Godhead as can be found in a man, so in Paul we find as much of Christ as can be found in a sinner. In him, that is, even in his body, dwelt the fullness of Christ.

Now there is nothing which helps us more to understand the true nature of Christianity than to see it at work in a human life. The essence of Christianity is that a man or woman or child can here and now receive the gift of eternal life. This life is in Christ, and it is achieved when Christ is given a free hand wholly to possess us, and when we allow Him to indwell us. So Rabindranath Tagore prayed: 'O God, make my life simple and straight like a reed for Thee to fill with music.' And when we see Christ fill a man or woman with His Spirit, His mind, we then know how Christianity works out in life.

When I go through times of religious doldrums, when the Christian faith seems more complex than clear and when it is not easy to see the relationship between theology and daily life, I sometimes pass in review before my mind's eye certain Christians who without doubt have the Spirit of Christ. There is A in a Dorset cottage, and B in a Lancashire cobbler's shop, and C a widow in a West Country town, and D a restaurant proprietor in Westminster, and E a Midland industrialist, and F an Oxford mathematician. These people are in Christ and Christ is in them. I cannot say that 'life was different in those days', because I have known them all 'in the flesh'. I cannot excuse myself by saying that they are inhumanly saintly, because they all have faults. And yet, in spite of human failings, they have arrived at the great end for which the whole creation was begun. They are the product of the work of Christ in human life. Such men and women as these have let Him into their lives, with no rooms or even cupboards locked to Him. Such saints, of this or any other age, make it easier for the rest of us to know what it means to be full of Christ.

This, then, is not a theme for an academic essay. This is of urgent practical concern. The world needs to see more Christians—full-blooded, down-to-earth, heavenly-minded Christians. 'The fault', said A. S. Peake, 'that the world has to find with Christianity is not a scientific one, not even an intellectual one. It is that Christians are so unlike Christ.' Many who want to be Christians need to see Christ born again in someone like themselves.

It is no exaggeration to say that St Paul is part of the Christian revelation, in the sense that he holds a key place in the offering of Christ to the world. It was Christ's will that He should take up His abode in all His twelve apostles. One failed and slammed the door, to his own eternal loss. It may well have been God's will that Paul should become twelfth man in the place of Judas—and that the Church was mistaken in falling back on a pagan practice of casting lots when Matthias was chosen. Whether that was so or not, St Paul knew himself to be an apostle in whom Christ chose to reveal Himself.

It is hard to see how the Christian revelation could have been complete if God had not answered the question: 'But how does the Gospel *work?*' The Bible begins on a practical note: 'In the beginning God made . . .'; and His final act is to make men. This act of God is not complete until a man is made complete through the work of Christ. It is this completion of the Gospel that we see in St Paul. He stands for all time as an example of the Christ-made, Christ-filled life.

We can suitably turn to this theme in Lent, because it is the time of year when we examine ourselves in the light of the Gospel, and when we acknowledge that we need more of Christ. It was Paul's deepest longing that Christ should be 'formed in him', that is, that Christ should have Paul as an outward expression of Himself to the world.

> *How will the lost know of Jesus,*
> *If they do not see Jesus in me?*

We turn then to Paul as a guide to see what it means for Christ to dwell in the heart by faith.

CHAPTER ONE

My Gospel

Now to him that is able to stablish you according to my
gospel . . . be the glory for ever (Rom 16$^{25\text{-}7}$)

PEOPLE ARE always looking for a man who is absolutely sure;
they are ready to follow a man who knows without doubt
where he is going; they will listen spell-bound to the man or
woman or child who is white-hot with conviction.

Yet there is a type of dogmatism which is infuriating. There
is a species of cock-sure, self-confident certitude which may
aggravate the listener rather than persuade and convince. A
man can over-state his case, or present it in such a way as to
suggest that you are a fool not to have hit on an idea which is
so obvious, or 'lay down the law' so that you resent domination
and sales-resistance sets in.

Now I believe that in presenting Paul and his Gospel to the
world, it has far too often happened that the preacher and
teacher have spoiled Paul's 'brief' for him. They have made
him sound over-confident in himself. In so doing, they have
injured not only Paul but Christ Himself. Paul was not concerned about being attractive; he had no illusions and never
expected people to call him 'a popular preacher', 'a magnificent figure of a man', 'the golden-voiced orator', 'the irresistible
advocate'. He never thought in terms of 'personal magnet-
ism'. Far from it! In a moment of frankness he admits that
his speech was 'rude' ('I may be no speaker', *NEB*) and he
quotes his readers' sneer at him, that his 'presence was weak
and his speech contemptible' (2 Cor 10^{10}, 11^{6}). But preachers
have sometimes made him seem self-opinionated, and because
Paul has been badly represented, many a listener or reader
has been annoyed with him or become allergic to his message.
For every one Christian who, being head over heels in love,

has said with 'Woodbine Willie', 'I cannot get to Jesus for the glory of her hair', there have been many more who have said: 'I cannot get to Jesus for the complexity of Paul's epistles.' And all the time we have at our disposal an interpreter to reflect the Light of the World if only we would use him. Paul wants to be heard in order that we may hear Him that sent him.

It is a great day in the life of a Christian when he realizes that Paul was one of God's greatest gifts to mankind, and most of all as the ambassador and mouthpiece of Christ. 'The means by which Providence raises a nation to greatness', said Edmund Burke, 'are the virtues infused into great men', and all humanity is enriched by what Christ did in the soul of St Paul. I shall never cease to thank God for having had a father who taught his children to think of Paul as a warm, virile, human, gentle, attractive, amusing, tough, Greatheart. What are we to make of it when Paul talks about 'my gospel'? The phrase sounds rather like a man who is selling 'My System' of health culture (by Sandow) or memory training (by Pelman)! You look for the twelve easy lessons which get more and more complicated as the course proceeds, so that what started as a quite good idea becomes intolerably complicated, grievous to be borne.

But Paul's Gospel is Christ. He has no idea in his head but Christ; he has nothing to sell but offers a free gift, and it is eternal life in Christ. In fact, Paul's Gospel is Christ's Gospel, and Christ's Gospel was Himself. We shall find as we proceed that what Paul teaches is the very echo of his Master's voice. The most valuable part of this book will lie in its many quotations from the New Testament, though I hope it will not deserve the criticism which the professor made of a volume upon which he had been asked to comment: 'This book is both good and original; unfortunately the parts which are good are not original, and the parts which are original are not good!' Paul will be much quoted, but as we look at his words we shall find that here is in fact the expression of the mind, if not of the very words, of Christ.

This brings us to an important fact and one which has been making a deep impression on me for some years. Although there are very few instances of exact quotations of the words of Jesus in the writings and speeches of St Paul, there is overwhelming evidence that Paul has so absorbed Christ's Gospel that he is in fact thinking Christ's thoughts after Him.

Let us look at this more closely. A man who is not in sympathy with you may quote you exactly, word for word. He is accurate and you cannot say that he has 'got you wrong', especially if he has made use of a concealed tape-recorder! But suppose he goes on to *interpret* you, so to speak, and attempts to give others a true impression of your mind and intention. You may not be so happy about this. You find that he gives a different slant to your opinions and motives. He distorts and twists. By his selection and presentation of your opinions, he may bring them into disrepute.

Now on the other hand suppose that a man in complete sympathy with you undertakes the task of reporting you. He knows what you are talking about, even if he has no mechanical record of your actual phrases. He has insight into your mind, which is more important than a *memoriter* record of your words. This man will report you fairly; in fact by his presentation of your case he may well add helpfully and constructively to what you have said.

It is exactly this which God intended to be the role of the New Testament evangelists in the exposition of the Word made flesh. Paul does not merely rattle off the phrases of Jesus and repeat what was being written and would later be completed with a supernatural perfection by the four evangelists. His is not merely a tape-recording of the Gospel. To be able to quote an authority is within the scope of a lawyer's clerk. But Paul does more than this. It is true that we shall find in his writings more quotations direct or indirect of the teaching of Jesus than many people imagine; it must also be true that words of Paul have sometimes been attributed to Christ and vice versa; Paul is often so reminiscent of Jesus that we do not stop to ask: 'Where have I heard this before?' But what is more impressive is that the whole spirit of his message breathes the Mind of Christ.

There can be little doubt that Paul had access in some form to collections of sayings of Jesus. (In Chapter 3 we shall discuss whether or not he saw Jesus in the flesh.) But in a sense Paul is the great archetype of those who are blessed because, not having seen, they have yet believed. The level at which the Gospel of Christ has penetrated Paul's being is far deeper than that of mere verbal repetition. This deep subliminal impact is most impressive.

It is a common thing for people to assimilate teaching without being able to give chapter and verse for their convictions. Take as an illustration the impact made on many lives by what thirty or forty years ago was called 'the New Morality'. There were some who could quote Havelock Ellis or D. H. Lawrence, either because they were in sympathy with them or merely students of current morals. But there were many more who had assimilated this advocacy of immorality without perhaps ever being able to quote a single sentence in support of their philosophy. If you had said: 'You are merely an echo of Havelock Ellis', with a blank look they might have replied: 'Never heard of him'; but the impact was there, deep and dangerous.

St Paul has been thoroughly indoctrinated with the Mind of Christ; he has been 'gospelized'. When he talks of '*his gospel*' he is not suggesting that he has worked out his own scheme of salvation. He is talking rather about the news he has to share with others, and that news is not Paul's ideas, but Christ Himself, and all that he has received through Christ.

He has made this Gospel completely his own, of course. 'Nothing anonymous can preach', said Cardinal Newman. Paul does not conceal the fact that it is he, Paul, the religious failure, ex-Pharisee of the Pharisees, ex-legalist, ex-persecutor of the Church, who is preaching. He is a living witness to the power of the Gospel he preaches. As Luther says: 'His word thunders whose life lightens.' Part of Paul's very Gospel is what the Gospel has done for Paul. But this makes him an all the more effective proclaimer of the message.

What *is* this Gospel which Christ proclaimed? Wise men—falsely so-called—claim that Paul has distorted it.

Jesus came preaching what He called 'the Gospel of the Kingdom of God' (Mark 1¹⁴). Paul says that God has translated us into the Kingdom of the Son of His love (Col 1¹³). Paul's Gospel is set within this vast framework of the fatherly rule of God. The Kingdom is a term which has been bandied about in Christian literature to cover almost every aspect of the life and activity of God. But this is understandable, since that is exactly what Jesus implied! The Kingdom of God is everywhere, the beginning and end of all that is. It is a far larger conception than the Church. Can we 'extend God's Kingdom', as we so often pray? What we can do is to persuade anarchists to acknowledge what is already a fact—that God sitteth upon the throne, be the earth never so unquiet.

How do men come to know consciously and trustfully that they live in this Kingdom of God's love?

There is a sense in which many besides the Christian evangelists open up the Kingdom of Heaven to those who will believe. The scientists (and we must remember that the word scientist is a generic term for men who dig in many corners of God's garden) are messengers of the Kingdom; whether they acknowledge a divine Creator or not, they are in fact uncovering the handiwork of God. Certain also of our poets can be said to be interpreters of the Kingdom of God in that they open our eyes to bits of life and, as expositors of our existence in some phase or other, teach us more of the God in whom we live and move and have our being. The teachers of morals and those who formulate the laws of mankind are, consciously or unconsciously, legislators in the Kingdom of God. They cannot make or unmake the laws of God, but by their pronouncements and formulations of codes of behaviour, they are saying in effect that in this way or that the life of mankind can best be maintained in order and tranquillity. Even the ordinary human parent is a servant of God's Kingdom in that

B

he is himself *in loco parentis*, in the place of the heavenly Father in caring for His children.

It is possible for such workers in God's Kingdom to have a zest in their calling which makes them aware that they are in their own way servants of the Word. I knew a brilliant naturalist who would come from his laboratory and play 'All things bright and beautiful' for children gathered round the piano, realizing that the 'world of science' was only another phrase for the Kingdom of God. Virgil and his *Georgics*, Wordsworth and his Prelude, or W. H. Davies and his Lyrics —irrespective of the authors' ignorance or vagueness about the Christian revelation—have laid hold of a bit of God's garment and said: 'Just look at this!' The law-givers and teachers of good behaviour like Solon and Socrates and Bacon have played their part in helping us to know the nature of God's Kingdom in men's lives. The fathers and mothers of the world have experienced something of the Kingdom in miniature in their own home and through the ages parents have felt a glow of pride that God has magnified them for His purposes in procreation. I saw one of our children born and the radiance on my wife's face was the light of the Kingdom of God. She was part of the great story of His unfolding love in human life.

But when you have said all this, you have not come within a hundred miles of 'the light of the Gospel of the glory of Christ, . . . the light of the knowledge of the glory of God in the face of Jesus Christ' (2 Cor 4[4, 6]).

For Christ and his apostles there is a depth of meaning in 'the Gospel of the Kingdom' which is only found by dipping into one particular well, and this well is Christ. The water there is so deep and for ever fresh that even Jacob's well (which was traditionally inexhaustible) becomes as so much dried-up earth. There is a Gospel of the Kingdom which is only to be found in Him who is the King's Son who came to open up the Kingdom of Heaven to all believers.

Jesus Christ and the Gospel in Him does not imply merely a set of ideas that men could have discovered for themselves.

He is in himself a mighty act of the great King. He is the
elder brother of God's fatherly rule, who has in fact and in
history come to reclaim the prodigals who are at large and
adrift. He was born of a woman, crucified by a procurator,
seen alive after death by witnesses, and these facts constitute
the good news of the Kingdom. No one can *make* you believe
this Gospel; you must take it or leave it.

The Gospel of Jesus is summed up in the phrase: 'The
Father hath sent me' (Jn 5³⁶). So it is for St Paul: 'God sending his own son in the likeness of sinful flesh' (Rom 8³). This is
the one and only Gospel which Paul can fitly call '*My* Gospel',
and everything else stems from it. Lloyd George one day at
breakfast said to J. C. Carlyle: 'An evangelist must have *one*
message.' For St Paul this was his one message, that God was
in Christ, reconciling the world unto Himself (2 Cor 5¹⁹). In
essence this Gospel is simple, though God forgive us we have
made it complicated at every turn. John Oman in speaking of
the simplicity of the Gospel says: 'The words which to the
Apostle Paul were plain everyday speech have become remote
and elaborate and technical—"God was in Christ" to him
meant simply the felt presence of the Father in One who was
perfectly His Son; to his interpreters it is a complex and
mysterious doctrine of Christ's Person.—"Reconciling the
world", which was simply turning men from enemies into
friends, is expounded by perplexing controversies about
prevenient grace—"not imputing trespasses" which was simply
the pardon which restores to fellowship in spite of offences,
is turned into difficult and forbidding theories of justification.'

No other Gospel was worth calling a Gospel. Other schemes
of salvation were to St Paul nothing but the wisdom of men.
Many of his contemporaries would rather have heard a message
about other things, about deliverance from political oppression
or release from social injustice or freedom from fear of evil
spirits. Men are often apt to estimate the real needs of the
world at far too shallow a level. A man in the Air Force once
told me that he thought the real tragedy of the war was that
it had come 'just at a time when we were getting going on

a decent civilization, holidays with pay and all that!' But
social security, or even demon security, is not man's deepest
need.

Paul knew better. There is one underlying need in every
age: that men shall hear '*The* Gospel', which is centred in the
person of Jesus Christ. All other concerns may be related to
this, but Christ is the core of the matter.

'My Gospel' when once it had dawned upon his soul, gave
Paul the motive and driving power for all his experience. The
tribute to Dr Luke Wiseman inscribed on a tablet in Birming-
ham Central Hall runs thus: 'He preached the assurance of
God's love in Jesus with the zest of high adventure.' This was
exactly true of Paul. God had visited his people and that visit
was to prove an eternal benison to mankind.

No one can proclaim the coming of God in Christ as a Gospel
(as distinct from a mundane historical or theological fact)
unless it has first gripped his own soul. He is not likely to cry,
'This is my story, this is my song', if he only considers the
fact of Christ to be on a par with the fact of Julius Caesar, or
the discovery of the wheel or the atom. But when once a man
knows that Christ is the key to the Kingdom of Heaven, he
knows that in offering Christ, he is dispensing riches unsearchable. A man who knows what the Gospel is about
counts all things loss for the excellency of the knowledge of
Christ Jesus, his Lord (Phil 3^8). The Gospel had given Paul a
soul to call his own, and 'What shall a man give', said Jesus,
'in exchange for his soul?' (Mt 16^{26}).

Let us notice, then, three things about Paul's Gospel:

(1) IT WAS NOT HIS OWN INVENTION

It was not his own philosophy, or formula for salvation. It
was not his own discovery or concoction. He says that the
Gospel he preached was not 'after man' (least of all himself).
'For neither did I receive it from man, nor was I taught it,
but it came to me through revelation of Jesus Christ' (Gal 1^{12}).
He had not hit upon it; it had hit him! It was not that he had
cried 'Eureka!'—as though he had discovered Archimedes'

principle. It was rather that he knew 'We have found the Messiah (which is, being interpreted, Christ)' (Jn 1⁴¹). We are completely misjudging Paul if we think of his religious experience as being subjective. The point about the great stories of conversion—for instance of Martin Luther or John Wesley—is that these men found a solution to the enigma of life outside themselves. They found it in the Gospel which confronted them. The fact of Christ was a solid rock fact for Paul, and when he proclaimed the Gospel it was with the complete assurance that a Saviour had come and been crucified, and His authenticity had been proved by an event of inescapable importance, the Resurrection. It is strange to think that man's confidence should rest in two holes in the ground—the place where they stood the Cross and the place where they laid His body.

Far from being a perverter of the Gospel, Paul had it as his one aim to ensure that the world heard the Gospel purely and simply. His expositions of what the dying and rising of Jesus mean to us must never conceal the fact that he was primarily concerned to report an event. He was not engaged in arguing about a philosophy of life. When Paul talks about 'my preaching' (1 Cor 2⁴) you will notice from the Revised Version margin that this means 'the thing preached'. The apostolic preaching was a definite pronouncement, a proclamation, not a statement of a case to be argued. 'Remember Jesus Christ, risen from the dead, of the seed of David, according to my gospel' (2 Tim 2⁸). Would that all preachers could remember this at all times—that the Christian message is not their presentation of truth or their opinions. How many a preacher would be saved from a constant struggle 'to get on to a good line', 'to find a message for Sunday', if he kept always in the forefront of his mind Paul's dictum that we preach not ourselves but Christ Jesus as Lord. The man who is always ferreting round in his mind for new ideas ends up like a poor old miser, turning over the same old coins in his box. But he who draws on the Gospel of Jesus Christ will continue to bring out of his treasure things new and old.

(2) AND YET THIS GOSPEL WAS HIS OWN

Every Christian is called upon at some time or other as a witness. Every disciple is an apostle. There is a sense in which every Christian can add to the corpus of epistles. Christ needs a great cloud of witnesses. Those who accept Christ as their Lord hear Him say to them: 'Go to thy house unto thy friends, and tell them how great things the Lord hath done for thee' (Mk 5¹⁹). Go and give your version of the New Testament in my blood. So Paul is in line with the will of his Master when he speaks time and again of 'My Gospel'. There is something special about each man's experience of Christ.

> Read all the libraries of saintliness,
> But think not God entire therein to scan;
> There still is something hid in God for thee,
> Unknown to any man.

I remember once standing before a portrait of Christ which was what is usually called 'advanced'. It was unconventional, so much so that I could not accept its challenge because of artistic conservatism. When I expressed disapproval and said, 'That's not Christ', the more experienced critic with me said: 'Nonsense; you've no right to say that. It may not be your view of Christ, but it is the Christ whom the artist has seen.'

The truth is that Christ is too great for any of us to know Him in all His fullness. We have no right to say that our view of the Gospel is the only one. The narrow-mindedness most to be deplored in the Christian Church is the rigidity of those who limit the Gospel to about half a dozen texts and phrases. If you use these, you know what the Gospel is! If you put the glory of redemption into other words, you do not pass muster! Out upon it! Read Samuel Rutherford, or Richard Baxter, or George Herbert or John Bunyan and watch for the continual variety of ways in which they speak of the Saviour, and you will know that here is a Face which cannot be painted in only one style of portrait.

The essential factor is that there should be a personal bond between Saviour and saved which is implied in Paul's phrase 'My Gospel'. When a Cornish servant-girl heard the well-known account of John Wesley's conversion at Aldersgate Street, she said it was the *me* and the *my* and the *now* which made all the difference. The wonder of Christ's work as Redeemer is that the same old story can be applied to such an infinite variety of lives, so that all men who accept his salvation feel that it is exactly what they need. It works for *anyone*.

Sidney Dark tells an amusing story in *Not Such a Bad Life*. In the last century there was a successful writer of plays called Pettit. They were all melodramas, variations on the same theme. One day at the Savage Club a friend greeted him to wish him good luck at the first night of the new rendering of the same plot. 'Hullo, Pettit, I hope the new play will be a success'; to which Pettit replied: 'Thanks, old chap, I think it will be; it always has been!'

Paul is able to go on through his ministry offering his Gospel to one sort of listener after another with complete confidence, knowing that when once it is heard (in the biblical sense of hearing) it will be effective. 'My Gospel' can become your gospel.

How? The Gospel becomes our own when we allow the full impact of Christ's death and resurrection to be reproduced in our own life. T. H. Green says, writing on 'Faith': 'The concern of the best Christian teachers has been, and, when they are wise enough to stop their ears against the clamours of scepticism, still is, not to win assent upon the evidence of the miraculous narrative of the Gospels . . . , but to bring their people to enact in their own hearts and lives the work which the creeds rehearse; not to convince them that Christ was miraculously born and died and rose again, but so to affect them that they shall die and rise again with Him and live as those to whom their sins have been forgiven and the gate of Eternal Life thrown open.'

(3) PAUL'S GOSPEL WAS WORTH DYING FOR

Paul believed that God had separated him to the Gospel of God (Rom 1[1]). He was set on 'ministering in sacrifice'

(Rom 15^{16}, *RV*m) the Gospel of God. He called Timothy to suffer hardship with the Gospel according to the power of God (2 Tim 1^8). He told the Corinthians that he did all things for the Gospel's sake that he might be a joint partaker thereof (1 Cor 9^{23}). Such a defence of the Gospel had been anticipated by Jesus who had steeled the hearts of his disciples to be ready to lose their lives for His sake and the Gospel's (Mk 8^{35}).

We are very near the bone here when we examine our own Christian life and witness in modern times. No one can easily assess how firmly he would hold on to any particular article of faith under duress. 'A man's true creed', said Bernard Shaw, 'is what he would be ready to die for.' Many a simple Christian who is quite unaware of being made in the martyr mould might well, if the test came, stand against the wall till his body fell limp before the machine-guns. For one thing we do not know what fortitude Christ could impart to us 'in that hour'. One of the most stalwart Christians I have known told me that she was sure that if Hitler had come, she would never have had sufficient courage in her convictions to go to a concentration camp. I myself feel sure that she would have had and was perhaps all the stronger for not being self-confident.

You need to have a very positive gospel based on tested convictions to be able to say with Paul, 'I am ready to go bound unto Jerusalem', and when we examine ourselves we find that much that we proclaim as the Christian Gospel is not a Gospel worth dying for. If our message is nothing more than self-cultivation in morality, then no wonder we are less confident and aggressive than Paul, who was not ashamed of his own Gospel because it was to him the power of God unto salvation.

The followers of Christ in any age are at their best when they know that it is the one central Gospel which is the chief thing about Christianity. We are not called to argue the other man down, but to lay down our own life for the Gospel.

Adolf Hitler probably never anticipated being quoted in a Methodist Lent Book, but it is worth while recording one of his wiser statements in *Mein Kampf:* 'The greatness of

Christianity did not arise from attempts to make compromises with those philosophical opinions of the ancient world which had some resemblance to its own doctrine, but from the unrelenting and fanatical proclamation and defence of its own teaching.'

For St Paul that teaching was nothing more or less than the Gospel.

CHAPTER TWO

My Mind

The law of my mind (Rom 7²³)

WE TURN now to examine more carefully the nature of Christ's impact upon Paul.

Paul had many ways of expressing his experience of Christ. One description which he gives of the Christian life is that he is *in Christ*. He is becoming part of that New Man, the reconditioned mankind which Christ is creating as He gathers men to Himself. This is perhaps an even vaster conception than Paul's claim that Christ was in him. You will find a full exposition of this theme in *A Man in Christ* by James Stewart, one of the great scholar-preachers of our generation. A Christian is one who is in Christ, as well as having Christ dwell in him.

Another of Paul's descriptions of the Christian life is that he is *with Christ*. This is a factor which must never be forgotten. We are called into the fellowship of Jesus Christ our Lord (1 Cor 1⁹). Christ does not obliterate personality. That is the fallacy of Buddhism, to aim at self-annihilation. Christ is still one who humbly asks: 'Lovest thou me?' and who promises: 'Lo, I am with you.' For St Paul life was a journey with Christ, right from the Damascus Road (where he was confronted not by a mere subjective impression, but by a person outside himself) through to the days when, as a prisoner under sentence of death, he said that Christ stood by him. We can only apprehend Christ through a glass, darkly. The veil of flesh now divides us from Him, but one day we shall be with Christ in a perfect fellowship, 'which is far better'.

Then again, a Christian's life is lived *for Christ*. He is dedicated to Christ's service as an offering. There is a sense in which Paul's devotion to Christ can be interpreted as hero-worship to the nth degree. The lover enjoys everything he undertakes for his beloved. The Christian's life has a purpose, and that is that he may be used to 'fill up' the honour and glory of Christ.

But our concern here is with that description of the Christian life which says that *Christ is in me*. Paul says categorically 'We have the mind of Christ'. Before we accuse him of presumption, let us remember that Paul is not talking here like one of those irritating pietists who speak as though they were personal private secretary to the Almighty; if you really want to know the official point of view, you must ask them! In this very passage Paul has quoted Isaiah 40: 'Who hath known the mind of the Lord, that he should instruct him?' When we start saying what God thinks we are always in great danger. We find so often that we are claiming His imprimatur on our own opinions. One wonders whether there is not a quiet voice in the High Court of Heaven: 'I never said any such thing.'

Paul does not claim to know all mysteries or to possess all knowledge. God's knowledge is too wonderful, it is high, we cannot attain to it. Here is no claim to omniscience. If Paul had presumed to know all things, he would have been guilty of the sin of Eden. He is not telling the Lord what to think. 'Who directed the spirit of the Lord? With whom did God take counsel? Who showed Him the way of understanding?' When he is unsure whether his own judgement is in line with the spirit of Christ, he is scrupulously careful to say so. When he is discussing marriage in relation to unbelievers, he is very careful to distinguish between 'permission' and 'commandment'; he says in one phrase: 'I give charge, yet not I, but the Lord . . .', but in another: 'To the rest say I, not the Lord: . . .' (1 Cor 7⁶⁻¹²); he is careful to say: 'I think I have the mind of the Lord.' It is very important this, to guard Paul against any charge of claiming infallibility. I may be befuddled by denominational prejudice, but I have never been able fully to understand the doctrine of papal infallibility. One thing I do know: whenever on numerous occasions I have asked a Roman Catholic friend to explain it to me, he has always been so anxiously careful to emphasize all the provisos and limiting clauses that I have been inclined to echo the visitor at the zoo looking into the camel's cage—'There ain't no such animal.' If one had put point-blank to Paul the question: 'Do you really think that because you have the Mind of Christ your judgement is inerrant?' I believe he would have laughed angrily. He would have laughed because the idea is ludicrous; he would have laughed angrily because the idea is blasphemous. We must walk humbly with our God all our days. Even though we strive with all our mind to search the deep things of God, we still may not understand Him aright.

Arthur Miller, in the preface to his collected plays, protests that none of his audiences has ever got him right! *All My Sons* was about loneliness, not the profit motive, or fathers and their sons; *The Crucible* was not a historical allegory on McCarthyism but a statement about conscience. Mr Miller, viewing this constant misrepresentation, writes of his 'sense of defeat'.

How often during His earthly life our Lord had to interpret His parables afresh privately. Are we sure that even now we always get the right interpretation? I remember once being allowed to attend a certain learned society of New Testament scholars in Cambridge, and hearing them disagree. I thought: 'Well, this is very encouraging; if these men cannot agree, I need not call myself a fool for not always being sure about the meaning of Jesus.'

The plain fact remains: 'We have the Mind of Christ' is one article in the creed of the Christian's faith. It is one expression of the mystery of grace, that God gives Himself to us with such condescension that the very thoughts of our heart are imparted by Christ himself.

This is not the place to go into the complex question of terminology used in the Bible for man's inward experiences. I should love to see a book written by one who is both a theologian and a physiologist on the terms that are used—the reins ('guts'), soul, bowels, heart, womb, belly, bones, and so on.

Whilst for us perhaps 'the mind' is the most easily grasped, it is not Paul's only phrase. He speaks of the heart and the understanding, the eyes of the mind, and there is a sense in which even his use of the word 'flesh' is sometimes descriptive of that part of us in which Christ condescends to dwell. Anyhow, whatever phrases he uses, the tremendous implications are the same, that what we think and feel can be part of the very Spirit of Christ within us.

'But this is mysticism,' we may say, 'and that is beyond us.' We are not the only ones to shy off mentally from anything that sounds remotely mystical! It has been one of my constant longings in preaching to be able to get through to those, especially men, who panic at the very suggestion of a Christian experience which might be called mystical. There they are in the gallery, the accounts clerk, the electrical mechanic, the chartered surveyor, the grocer. Their life is beset with *things*. It is not that they are sensual or materialistic, but their lives are a constant trade in matter-of-fact, down-to-earth ponder-ables. They understand rates, and bus fares. They can handle their mowing machines or their carburettors; they can follow a quite involved political argument on economics or race relations. They can even grasp abstractions like kindness, or decency, or injustice. But when it comes to mystical talk about 'Christ in me' or 'having the Mind of Christ' a certain blankness or mental nervousness overtakes them.

But Paul would have us believe that this mind which was in Christ Jesus is not only for him but for us all. Christ's Mind must be in all His followers; indeed, 'Christ's Mind', he says, 'must be among you', that is, in all your relationships with one another.

But can one man take over another man's mind? It may help us to understand the phrase if to begin with we remember some of the ways in which we constantly use the word 'mind' in common speech. Here are three of them:

(1) We say: '*So it is your mind that* ....' By this we mean that on the basis of the *words* you have just spoken I under-stand that this, or this, is implied. Am I interpreting you

rightly? In other words, have I your mind? So St Paul would say quite simply (without at the moment any high theory of a mystical indwelling) that we have Christ's mind. We should start with such sayings of Jesus as we can understand; we should let these sink into our mind. We should listen to the psalmist: 'Thy word have I laid up in my heart'; 'I will meditate in Thy precepts' (Ps 119[11, 15]). 'Thy law is within my heart' (Ps 40[8]). We should listen to the Lord speaking through Moses: 'These words which I command thee this day shall be upon thine heart' (Deut 6[6]). Jesus said: 'Ye are clean because of the word which I have spoken unto you' (Jn 15[3]). We should begin here. Let the words of Christ be constantly in our mind. We must never rank the words of Jesus more highly than His deeds. But we must not forget how great an emphasis He placed on His disciples' hearing what He said and remembering it. St Paul says: 'Let the word of Christ dwell in you richly' (Col 3[16]).

The trouble is that we often cannot understand the harder parts of the teaching of Jesus because we have not really tried to assimilate the easier.

(2) Or we may say of a person: '*You can see the direction in which his mind is working. . . .*' That is, we have taken note of his *behaviour* and *actions*, and this leads to certain deductions. He behaved like this, or that, because he wanted to show his confidence in us, or his disapproval. The girl who notices a young man's attention fixed upon her is perhaps very glad to see the way his mind is working! Similarly (and here again let us not panic, but be as matter-of-fact as we like!), we must look at Jesus and follow in our mind's eye the plain account of the story of Jesus of Nazareth. We must not attempt to be medieval mystics transfixed in an ecstatic gaze. One day we may see it all through Wordsworth's 'Veil of Ecstasy', but to begin with we must just read what happened. We must read the treatises 'concerning all that Jesus began both to do and teach until the day in which He was received up' (Acts 1[1-2]). We must follow His tracks to Calvary, and shut out all other thoughts while we hear Him cry: 'Father forgive them.'

We can see the way His mind is working. In our own mind we must think of Christ and think hard.

(3) Or yet again we may say: '*I know it would be his mind* . . . .' This may well refer to someone thousands of miles away from us, or someone whom we have not seen for years. It may even be someone who has died long ago. What do we imply?— that we have such an insight into a person's beliefs and judgements that we know exactly how he would react to any given situation. Many of us have known, for instance, precisely the sort of funeral arrangements to make for a loved one even though they may not have left behind any detailed instructions. All this is partly a matter of deduction, partly that we have caught their spirit and outlook and temperament. It is this sort of process which has been at work to create a Christian conscience on many a problem about which Christ said nothing specific at all. But we can say with confidence, for instance: 'I know it would be the mind of Christ that children of five should not be sent up hot chimneys, that women from Africa should not be shipped as slaves to the West Indies, that men should not gamble away their livelihood.' The social betterment of mankind as long as history lasts will depend on those who grasp and apply the Mind of Christ in their own generation.

Now let it also be said, and in no uncertain terms, that the impact of Christ's mind on us is in a very different category from any other experience we know. It is not merely that we take over Christ's point of view. There is a divine dimension here. He is a living supernatural Spirit, and an act of divine mercy takes place when He allows us to think His thoughts after him. But I do not believe that we should begin at that level. We should at least start at a place where our understanding moves with confidence and clarity.

To return to the accounts clerk and electrical mechanic with their allergy to mysticism, it is right to remind them how agile and fertile their mind can be when they choose. I always share with such men my own frailty. 'Look here,' I say, 'when I choose to use it, this thing that I am conceited enough to call a mind can be prolific and productive. Talk about a repertory theatre producing a play a week! When I give my mind to it, I can be the author, producer, stage manager, director, choreographer, artist in décor and costume, and produce an incredible variety of dramas (many of them unfit for public presentation).'

For St Paul the mind is that part of us which does the thinking and feeling. If we could tell exactly how a thought passes from one mind to another, we should be able to get a professorship in any university we chose. Here is a deep mystery into which many of the greatest thinkers of the human race have delved. But let us have a try. How does a thought come to us? One way is for someone to say something to us—words transmitted by speech or writing. So St Paul would say that the mind of Christ reaches us because we have heard what we have been told. This explains his constant emphasis on preaching: How shall they have the mind of Christ unless they hear; how shall they hear without a preacher? (Rom 10[14]). There is a dreadful logic about this, and that one text is like an electric charge in the batteries of many a Mission House.

Another way a thought can be born is by our achieving the consummation of a marriage of two thoughts, so that a new thought is born. This process is constantly at work in our minds if you notice. This and this put together make that. Now Jesus was constantly calling forth this activity in the minds of His hearers. How often Jesus says: 'How think ye?' Listen to this story and put it alongside your own experience of life and draw your own conclusions. The mind of Christ is constantly brought to birth in the life of a Christian as we wed His words to our own life.

Or again, yet another more mysterious way that a thought can come to us is by direct transference. No serious student of the human mind now doubts the fact of telepathy. One mind in complete sympathy with another can give or receive direct impressions. At the highest level of all it is our faith that the Spirit of God can be in direct communication with the spirit of man. St Paul would have us be in no doubt whatsoever that he and the Lord were in direct intercommunion. In fact, if we query this, we are hard-pressed at every turn in the Bible. 'The Lord said to me', 'I cried unto the Lord and said . . . .' Are all these just out-pourings of imagination and auto-suggestion? No, we make a mockery of Christian experience if we stop short of full communication between Christ and the human soul. If we never 'expect a word' from Christ we are not likely to hear one. The very fact of our unbelief will be as definite an act as though we had stopped up our physical ears. It all depends on whether or not we believe in the work of the Spirit who is the means of communication between us and God.

The Mind of Christ, like the phrase 'the Word of God', is a wide and glorious term. His mind reaches us through the words and deeds recounted in the Bible and our personal deductions from them, but also His mind enters our mind when in expectant faith we cry, 'Lord, speak to me'.

> To Thee, inseparably joined,
>   Let all our spirits cleave;
> O may we all the loving mind
>   That was in Thee receive!
> This is the bond of perfectness,
>   Thy spotless charity;
> O let us (still we pray) possess
>   The mind that was in Thee!

The full impact of Christ's mind is only felt by those who are ready to let Him fill the very recesses of their sub-conscious as well as conscious thought. 'He giveth unto his beloved *in sleep*' (Ps 127², *RV*m). I should feel far more confident in calling myself a saint, if, for instance, I *dreamed* about Christ. To my shame I cannot recollect ever having done this. It was a very godly man, of whom it was said:

> His dreams are faithful to his prayers
> And follow with closed eyes the path of love.

C

Is it too banal a thing to say that we have not the Mind of Christ more fully because we quite simply do not think enough about Him? A little girl once said to her mother: 'I should love to look at you all the time, if there were not so many other interesting things to look at.' A Christian cannot begin too soon, or go on too long just looking at Jesus until His mind is in him.

This was the sampler I once read in a doctor's waiting-room:

> *Jesus, permit Thy gracious Name to stand*
> *As the first efforts of an infant's hand,*
> *And whilst the fingers on the canvas move,*
> *Engage her tender heart to seek Thy love.*
> *With Thy dear children let her have her part,*
> *And stamp Thy holy image on her heart;*
> *And day and night be it her constant care*
> *To guard and keep Thy sacred image there.*
>
> 1817. Olive Furber,
> Aged 8.

If we are to have the mind of Christ, we must read, mark, learn and inwardly digest Him in all His words and works. As Paul Bull says: 'We study the truth in order that we may possess it; we meditate upon the truth in order that it may possess us.'

CHAPTER THREE

My Face in the Flesh

As many as have not seen my face in the flesh (Col 2^1)

As FAR back as I can remember, it was drilled into me that
a Christian must have a personal experience of Christ. But
also as far back as I can remember this phrase switched on a
warning bell in my mind. 'A definite personal experience of
Jesus Christ', they said. But how can one 'experience' an
individual of bygone days? Study, yes; hero-worship, yes;
keeping constantly in mind, yes. But to have an experience
of someone means to meet them, talk with them, and receive
from them their personal reactions to yourself as an individual.
I do not feel that I have had a personal experience, for instance,
of Mr Gladstone, whom I have not seen; nor even of Mr
Churchill, whom I have seen but without any element of
personal encounter.

Here, I am sure, is 'the jackpot question' of the Christian
claim. How can you have an experience of Christ without
having met Him in the flesh? How can I, living in this century, be linked with one who lived in the first century?

We in our generation sometimes excuse ourselves for being
too obsessed with the physical aspects of life. We blame the
physicist, the biologist and all the other -ologists for making
us very aware of matter. And we tend to use this as an excuse
for not arriving at a simple child-like trust in the field of
religion—as much as to say: 'You know, it's terribly difficult
when one knows so much!' We have half-assimilated and
under-digested a certain amount of scientific method in our
thinking: we have been conditioned to suspect any assertion for
which there is no verifiable proof, often overlooking the fact
that there are many different ways of verifying evidence.

Every generation in its turn is cumbered with much serving

of man's physical nature. The saints had eyes in their head and knew what it was to be tempted by the world and the flesh as well as by the devil! We are grossly mistaken if we imagine that Christianity is only for those who possess a refined spirituality so that it is liable to escape the man who grows up in an atmosphere of scientific materialism. Christianity is not merely the holding of communion with the Spirit of God in a rarefied atmosphere of weightless detachment. It is of all religions the most 'earthed'. It can fit into every century. The faith which is rooted in the man born of a woman can still be lived by men who are tempted by women, and the Lord who turned water into wine can still be the Saviour of the analytical chemist in the research laboratory.

We must not deceive ourselves that there is anything specially different about us because we find it hard to 'see' Christ *by faith*. Let us ask a direct question. Have we ever followed through logically the implication of the very human longing to have seen Jesus? We often fail to work out what would happen if we were given a free hand in God's scheme. There are some who say: 'If only I could have one straight-forward look at Christ, one personal conversation, a direct contact in the matter-of-fact meaning of the term, I could then more easily form my own judgement about Him.' But do we really wish that His hands had been placed on our head, or that His arms had been thrown around us? How far in all honesty can we say that it would be easier to believe in Him if we had a face-to-face encounter? On one point alone: how should we expect to see Him dressed? This is not really a trivial question. It was the very humanity of His clothing (a carpenter's apron, not even a prophet's leather girdle) which put a veil over the eyes of many. Do we seriously wish that Jesus were our physical contemporary? What if we saw Him being interviewed, not by Pharisees from Jerusalem but by John Freeman or Archbishop Heenan? What if we saw Him not as a carpenter but as the proprietor of a shop for do-it-yourself materials? Are we sure that we should leap readily to the conclusion that here is the Lord of Glory in whom dwells the fullness of God in a body? Let us face this question honestly, and when once we have given an answer, let us not go back on it.

A lot of this talk about 'if only I could see Him' is escapist. St Thomas is a patron saint for many of us, and largely for this reason, that his faith in the Incarnation and in the risen Christ came only after much heart-searching and after a tremendous leap of worship towards Him whose hands had taken both an oar and the print of the nails. When Jesus said, 'Blessed are they that have not seen', He used the word 'blessed' as He had used it in the Beatitudes. Those people are to be envied who have not the exacting mental conflict involved in seeing a carpenter and saying: 'This is the Christ.' We are to be envied who though not having seen His face in the flesh with the eyes in our head, yet can say that we know and believe by faith that the Lord of life is come. This faith is not mere speculation. It is built on the basis of multiple evidence—history and testimony and, most of all, the inner witness of His Spirit in our own heart.

It is time we turned again to St Paul. I want in this chapter to make one simple but important point about him and then elaborate it. I believe that Paul represented a unique stage of transition in Christ's relationship with mankind. He stands between those who were the intimate associates of Jesus in the days of His flesh, who heard and saw and handled the Word of Life (1 Jn 1[1]), and the rest of us in mankind who know Him by faith, but not by sight.

It may surprise us that Paul seems so little concerned about Christ's earthly life, other than His death and resurrection. There are various reasons for this: for one thing, these details were being collected and preserved by others. Paul would know of this and it is noteworthy that from time to time he refers to words of Jesus, but does not feel it necessary to quote them in full (Gal 6[2], 1 Cor 7[10], 9[14]). (We must never imagine that Paul was able to hold in his hand a copy of the four gospels in basic Greek to which he could refer his readers!) But it was not Paul's purpose to present a systematic *Life and Teaching of Jesus.* His letters are occasional, personal, and in the main, 'bitty'. They are all the more authentic evidence for being so.

Paul may or may not have seen Jesus. We cannot say for certain, for instance, whether the *we* in 'Even though we have known Christ after the flesh' (2 Cor 5¹⁶), means Paul himself or the human race as a whole. But here are one or two things to consider. He was so strict a Pharisee of the Pharisees that it is hard to imagine his being able to keep out of so urgent a controversy as the Case of the Nazarene. He had obviously developed a deep violent hatred and his inquiring mind could not have remained disinterested on so big an issue. He was regularly at Jerusalem, and probably a member of the Sanhedrin, and it is more than likely that his visits coincided with at least one of the visits of Jesus. But a great deal of this is conjecture. When he said, 'Have I not seen Jesus our Lord?' (1 Cor 9¹) it is hard to assess whether he was referring to the Damascus Road encounter, or to some previous meeting in the flesh. Similarly, when he said, 'I received of the Lord' (1 Cor 11²³), he might easily be using the phrase as we ourselves might say: 'Jesus gave us the Lord's Prayer.'

Dr Anderson Scott, and many with him, come down on the side of Paul's having actually met Jesus. He suggests that Paul's vivid reference to 'the blood' may be due to the fact that he had seen Jesus crucified and that he may even have been present at the Sanhedrin at the time of the trial. Dr Scott also quotes James Hope Moulton: 'Paul was in Jerusalem during the central act of human history, and it was then that he became humanly acquainted with Christ.' But this is still debatable and Paul certainly never based his authority on this type of contact with Jesus.

The one sure fact of which we can be confident is that Saul of Tarsus was up to the neck in the religious situation which Jesus had produced; he is not of another generation outside the events of which the four gospels speak. He stands alongside the other apostles as their contemporary, never allowing himself to be treated as a young interloper who has no authority. There are signs in the letters to the Corinthians and to the

Galatians that he is a little sensitive about being considered
inferior to those who had been so intimately near to Jesus.
They had witnessed His baptism, transfiguration and arrest.
One of them had actually lain back on Christ's breast at the
supper table. They had shared in His intimate conversation.
But Paul has his own special niche.

As arch-persecutor of the first followers of the Way, he had
ample opportunity to gather a large amount of detailed evidence. He would have made a superb Queen's Counsel, and
it was first-hand and not third-hand evidence that he was
sifting. If Paul had lived fifty years later, he would have
been much more suspect as a Christian authority. There used
to be a saying: 'I have danced with a man who has danced with
a girl who danced with the Prince of Wales.' When fifty years
had elapsed after the resurrection of Jesus there must have
been many who would claim that they had an uncle who had
met a woman who had talked with a cured leper who had been
healed by Jesus! If we cannot say with absolute certainty that
Paul and Jesus met face to face, it can be said categorically that
Paul was only too closely linked, often by chains and fetters,
with those who had been the actual companions and followers
of the Lord.

He had heard the testimony of Stephen, not only in the
public court, but quite possibly as well in personal conversation. When Stephen was martyred, did Paul's better nature
know, as the centurion at the foot of the Cross had known,
that he had been in the presence of the Son of God, whose
face was reflected in Stephen's? As Paul took up the martyr's
clothes, which had been laid at his feet, did one part of him
long to gamble his life away for Christ? Immediately after his
Damascus Road vision, Paul was in close fellowship with one
who must have been a wonderful Christian—Ananias, the
King's Messenger Extraordinary. Fancy being chosen by the
Lord to be the first counsellor to deal with Saul of Tarsus in
that inquiry room in Straight Street Damascus! I wish we
had a full report of what passed between them.

St Paul never looked on himself as just an ordinary

Christian; it was not a question of humility or pride, but fact, that he had been given a special role to play. Perhaps he was born rather late—as a baby who arrives in a family when you think there are going to be no more children (which is one meaning of the phrase 'one born out of due time'—1 Cor 15[8]) —but Paul has no doubt about the special nature of his contact with Christ. He cannot emphasize enough that the Lord has *appeared* to him. His conversion story is repeated and referred to again and again. (Incidentally, it is always worth noting anything which is reiterated in the Bible. Biblical repetition, unlike ours, is not caused by verbosity, or by having nothing else to say, or by lazy proof-reading!) St Paul's contact was special and unusual.

The reason is this: between the days of Pentecost and the age-long story of the Christian Church, Paul was vouchsafed an individual encounter with the Risen Christ; but—and herein lies Paul's usefulness to us all—that initial experience led on to a relationship with Christ which was to be of a quite different order. After all, before the Damascus Road, even if Paul did meet Jesus of Nazareth, there was not any love in Paul's eyes, and you cannot really know anyone whom you do not love.

What is more important for us is that that special visitation was followed by years of life with Christ *by faith alone*. So far as we know, Paul did not keep looking for a repetition of such an encounter. Once in a lifetime was enough! R. J. Knowling (in *The Testimony of St Paul in Christ*) says: 'No doubt the life of St Paul had points of contact with that of many a visionary; but the Apostle's life is not dependent upon any ecstatic conditions: it is rather a firm, unruffled, confident life in the Spirit, i.e. in Christ.'

Paul was content to accept Christ's terms of friendship. 'We walk by faith,' he says, 'not by sight' (2 Cor 5[7]). And thereby Paul, along with his fellow Apostles, after the Resurrection, became the first generation of those who bring into use that latent faculty in every man, the eye of faith.

What of ourselves? I believe there are times when we are

more certain than at others that we are near to the living
Christ. Let us never doubt these moments, and never forget
them. We should record and remember every Bethel. John
Bunyan, in one of the most perfect passages of writing in
English literature, his letter to his children at the beginning of
Grace Abounding, says:

'My dear children, call to mind the former days and years of
ancient times: remember also your songs in the night, and
commune with your own hearts. Yea, look diligently and
leave no corner therein unsearched, for that treasure hid, even
the treasure of your first and second experience of the grace of
God towards you; remember, I say, the word that first laid
hold upon you; remember your terrors of conscience and fear
of death and hell; remember also your tears and prayers to
God—yea, how you sighed under every hedge for mercy!
Have you never a hill Mizar to remember? Have you forgot
the close, the milkhouse, the stable, the barn, and the like,
where God did visit your souls?'

But in the main, our companying with Christ is on the
assurance of faith. Others may be mystified by our claim,
but the Lord is at hand!

A little while ago, I went one evening to a Lyons' Corner
House with a friend. Just before we entered he slipped down
the road to buy a paper. When I had sat down alone and the
waitress had come, I said: 'May we have some coffee, please?'
She looked at the empty chair on the other side of the table
and said 'How many are there of you?' I said: 'Oh, *two!*' I
suppose it is true to say that when you meet a Christian, you
meet two people, though you cannot see the Other.

Our life with Christ is one of trust, putting to the test the
things we cannot see. He would have it so. And we must
have it so. If we let Him, He is able to make His Presence
felt.

CHAPTER FOUR

My God

I thank my God through Jesus Christ. . . . (Rom 1⁸)

THERE WAS once a home where Father was a Methodist and Mother was a Quaker. One day, in the nursery, one child was overheard saying to another: 'Whose God do *you* worship—Mummy's or Daddy's?'

Children have a way of penetrating to the bone and marrow of a problem. Our religion can easily be of such a stamp that we give the impression that we have a particular brand of Deity of our own. Men speak of God as though He were their own possession, as though He were clay in their hand. This is evidenced not only in primitive man. If we were to collate all the phrases that we ourselves have ever used such as 'I can't believe in a God who . . . ', 'There's one thing I am certain of, that God never . . . ', 'You can be quite sure God always . . .' we might find ourselves confronted with a God such as never was on land or sea, let alone in Heaven.

It is obvious that if Paul is to justify his claim that he has the Mind of Christ, he must convince us that his conception of God has Christ's full authority. The purpose of this chapter is to show that Paul was so filled with the spirit of Christ that all his thoughts had become integrated into the character of God revealed to us by Jesus Christ. Paul had no ready-made Christian theology in which he could take a diploma (M.Th. Arabia!) He had never read Augustine or Aquinas or Dodd or J. B. Phillips—how *did* he manage? Well, the answer is: By superimposing the face of the Mediator upon all that he had ever thought about the Lord Jehovah. He did it not by 'montage'—the method by which photographers can add another figure to their picture. It came about through a new revelation, whereby the glory of God was revealed in the face of Jesus Christ.

(1) GOD IS ONLY TO BE FULLY KNOWN THROUGH JESUS

Here then is the first thing—that Paul's doctrine of God assumes and always accepts the claim of Jesus that no man cometh unto the Father but by His appointed Intermediary. The name 'Mediator' is an almost technical term—though the idea behind it is not technical but gloriously human with all the warmth of a great act of grace. Outside the Epistle to the Hebrews, the only occurrence of the word in the Bible is in 1 Timothy 2[5]: 'There is one God, one mediator, himself man, Christ Jesus.' This conception, however, is the very heart of the teaching of Jesus. It was the central core of His offer to the world that if we receive Him, then we receive Him that sent Him. St John says: 'He that hath the Son hath the life'—not only life in the sense of a way of living, but the Life of God Himself.

Jesus Himself says: 'He that hath seen me hath seen the Father.' I once heard Gipsy Smith say: 'Give me a child for a quarter of an hour and I will tell you what sort of parents he has.' A scholar in an East End Sunday School may not have been a conventional Bible commentator, but he was very near the theology of the New Testament when he said: 'Jesus was a chip of the old block.'

Jesus is the answer to man's age-long yearning for a Mediator. Men have longed for a Mediator in the person of the prophet (who shall bring God to us?)—and in the person of the priest (who shall raise us up to present us before God?). This briefly is the dual work of Jesus Christ. We love God because He first loved us and sent His Son. We have *access* to God (Rom 5[1, 2])—that is Paul's more common word corresponding to Mediator. We have peace with God because we have had access to Him by faith through our Lord Jesus Christ. He is the door of the sheep. It is through Christ that we have 'our access in one Spirit unto the Father'. We have boldness and access in confidence through our faith in him (Eph 2[18]).

To Paul the Christian all this was everyday speech, but to Saul of Tarsus it would have been blasphemous heresy. Yet there is no doctrine of God bearing Christ's authority which does not begin by stating that there is only one Mediator between God and us.

(2) GOD IS THREEFOLD IN NATURE

This brings us to the next factor, that the nature of God as revealed by Jesus and expounded by Paul is a threefold nature. Leonard Hodgson has concisely put this into a sentence: 'The Christian seeks to find and to do the will of the Father with the companionship of the Son through the guidance and strength of the Holy Spirit.' Paul's almighty Lord Jehovah is now the God who has approached us and whom we approach through Jesus, and who gives us His ever-present comforting Spirit. The doctrine of the Trinity is of course only a man-made formula. St Augustine said: 'It is not that we have the right words, but that we can think of no better.' It is man's way of explaining the nature of a God too full of mystery for words. But the facts which the doctrine of the Trinity tries to express lie behind every word of Jesus and every writing of St Paul. Woe betide us if we do not in these days, and the sooner the better, hammer home more dogmatic teaching about the Holy Trinity. If we proclaim a unitarian God, we cannot claim to have the mind of Christ.

In the chapel of Wesley House, Cambridge, you will find a pictorial representation of the Holy Trinity in the mural paintings. The splendour and glory of the invisible God is represented in a blaze of gold in the apse and the Spirit of God streams out in rays of golden light down the sides of the chapel, illuminating and warming all the life of man in his everyday pursuits. But also coming out from this golden glory is the figure of One like unto the Son of Man, the person of Christ, comprehensible and clear, stretching out His hand to the humanity whom He has come to join. The family of man-kind is pictured in a man bowed down with anxiety, and a mother who half-apprehends, and a child who is trustingly holding out his hands to the coming One.

This the three-fold nature of God, Father, Son and Spirit,

implicit in the teaching of Jesus and embedded in the thought of St Paul, is all the more impressively expressed in that it is not neatly and nicely defined in technical terms. St Paul's phrases glide into one another—God the Father, the Spirit of God, the Spirit of Jesus, the Lord. We notice (in Rom 8^{1-17} for instance), that Paul does not speak of God the Holy Spirit as an objective entity in a formulated doctrine, as later theologians tend to describe Him. Everything Paul describes is a matter of personal experience, and he moves quite naturally from one Person of the Trinity to another—as indeed 'the simple Christian' does to this day, provided his piety is well grounded in the New Testament! Paul speaks of the 'Spirit of God' (the Father) and 'the Spirit of Christ' and 'Christ', and then again of 'the Spirit of Him that raised up Christ', as if all these expressions were identical; and elsewhere he prays that the Father will strengthen his readers by His Spirit, in order that Christ may dwell in their hearts and they may be filled with the fullness of God.

Where the Spirit is, Christ is; and where Christ is, God the Father is. The action of one Person of the Trinity involves all the Persons. If the Father creates, He creates through the Son and by the Spirit. If the Son redeems, the redemption proceeds from the Father and is effected in the Spirit. If the Spirit sanctifies, it is from and in both the Father and the Son.

Paul wrote with uninhibited freedom, speaking from his own experience of the all-round work of God, Father, Son and Holy Spirit. He lived in the time of Apostolic orthodoxy before the days when men tip-toed through the paths of theology, afraid of stepping on a land-mine of heresy! But all that he said is reminiscent of Jesus, who at one moment is calling us to worship Him and Him that sent Him and Him whom the Father would send in His name.

(3) GOD IS OUR LOVING FATHER

St Paul in his everyday thoughts of God and in moments of intimate correspondence did not think cumbrously in the grand manner. For Paul, God is Abba, Father (Rom 8^{15}; Mk 14^{36}).

The Spirit of Jesus had so entered into his heart that he was able to say quite naturally 'Father'. God is now 'with us' through Christ by the Spirit, and all this is the very substance of Christ's doctrine of God. One is constantly impressed with the way in which Paul is aware of the friendship of God and speaks reassuringly of God's gracious care. It is not that the great I AM has changed His nature, but rather that He is now the great I-AM-WITH-YOU. Paul had so caught the spirit of sonship from Jesus that he knew himself to be a child of God as he had never known it before.

You can be someone's child without knowing who your father is. So everyone is God's child, but not everyone knows himself to be such. 'It is a paradox that God is "Father" of all men, but not all men are His sons' (C. H. Dodd). It is the work of God's Spirit to bring this fact home to our hearts. Living under the tyranny of sin, we are in the terrible condition where Christ can say to us: 'Ye are of your father, the devil.' The very image of God is erased when we fail to love our enemies as He does, or to be merciful as our Father is merciful. But the Spirit of the God who made us is able also through Jesus Christ to renew our true nature and grant us adoption. Now this word 'adoption' is reputed to be as common as any in Greek inscriptions of the Hellenistic era, and would be quite familiar to Paul's Gentile readers, though not to his Jewish compatriots. It was a common practice in the Roman world for a wealthy man with no children of his own to adopt a slave or an orphan. This child might know a father for the first time.

Paul's gospel, then, concerning the nature of God includes this theme that we who have been slaves under the tyranny of the Law can pass to 'a proud inspiring consciousness of being admitted into God's family, adopted as sons, and this unlocks our lips in tender filial appeal' (Sanday and Headlam). Two voices blend: the voice of the Holy Spirit, who brings to our remembrance all that Jesus said about the fatherhood of God, and our own consciousness, asserting that we truly are children of God. This awareness of sonship stimulates our speech as in childhood, so that we are enabled to say the first affectionate prayers to our Father. It is by the Spirit we are enabled to cry: 'Abba, Father.'

Paul's use of 'Abba, Father' has been variously interpreted. It has been thought that it may be a veiled reference to the Lord's Prayer, or just a bit of Aramaic which the early Church had retained in its public worship (much as we have kept such phrases as Hallelujah, Te Deum, Kyrie Eleison or Amen). It is more likely, however, that it is Paul's way of holding on in memory to the most common opening phrase of Christ's devotions, which had made such an impression on the apostles that they constantly spoke of it (as for instance they had remembered his 'Be of good cheer!' and 'Peace!'). What matters most, however, is that Paul has taken over quite naturally from Jesus the truth that God is our father, as we see in other expressions of his, such as 'God our Father' (a very common impressive phrase), 'the Father of mercies', 'the Father of our Lord Jesus Christ'. People who say that when they read Paul they feel as though he were speaking about a different God from the Father of Jesus, must have been nodding when they have been reading such phrases.

St Paul, when he speaks of God, always speaks in the same tender and confident terms as Jesus does. God is the creator who has made us and who daily provides for us. In Him we live and move and have our being. As Jesus says: 'Be not anxious . . . your heavenly Father knoweth' (Mt 6$^{25, 32}$), so St Paul bids his friends at Philippi: 'In nothing be anxious; but in everything by prayer and supplication . . . let your requests be made known' (Phil 4^6). It was Jesus who first drew men's attention to the fact that '*worry*' is a sin. It is a sin because it is a symptom of distrusting the fatherly goodness of God. It was this fatherly goodness which sustained our Lord through every trial He faced, and which was the basis of all Paul's confidence.

(4) GOD IS OUR HOLY JUDGE

The kindly Father, however, is not the whole picture of Christ's portrayal of God. Lest anyone imagine that the kindliness of

God has no corresponding shadow, let us remember a saying of Paul's: 'Observe the kindness and the severity of God' (Rom 11^{22}, *NEB*). One of the most heinous sins possible to man is the sin of presumption, and this is not only, in the sense in which it is used by Greek authors, a matter of intellectual pride, but also a matter of the practical attitude of forgetful insolence. It is a sin to take all God's goodness for granted. It could be said that in modern times we have implanted in the minds of our fellows in so-called Christian countries the thought of the goodness and the indulgence of God. To this extent the gospel has got across, but this very knowledge of God's kindliness may lead men to forget that the God who has the first word in our creation, and the continuing word in our preservation, has also the last word in our judgement. George MacDonald says: 'Lest it be possible that any un-childlike soul might, in arrogance and ignorance, think to stand upon his rights *against* God and demand of Him this or that after the will of the flesh, I will lay before such a possible one some of the things to which he has a right. He has a claim to be compelled to repent, to be hedged in on every side; to have one after another of the strong sharp-toothed sheepdogs of the great Shepherd sent after him, to thwart him in any desire, foil him in any plan, frustrate him of any hope, until he come to see at length that nothing will ease his pain, nothing make life worth having, but the presence of the Living God within him.'

We do a disservice to our neighbour if we paint a picture of God that is soothing. The God and Father of our Lord Jesus Christ is the God who spared not His own Son, and the over-powering sense of the majesty of God which St Paul had inherited as a Jew had not been obliterated, but if anything heightened by the sterner words in the teaching of Jesus. Our Saviour is not only the meek Lamb, but also the Lion of Judah. He is one who calls harlots His friends, but who also calls a king a fox. He does not only take children's sticky hands into His, but also a whip of small cords. Something goes wrong with all our devotion unless we take pains to enrich

our picture to include as much as is comprehensible to us of
the fullness of God who is the God both of Sinai and of
Olivet. To St Paul, as to his Master, God is our Judge—our
'Once and Future' Judge. 'God knoweth your hearts' (Lk 16^{15}),
Jesus had said to the Pharisees. 'He that searcheth the hearts
knoweth' (Rom 8^{27}), says Paul. The day will come, he says,
when God shall judge the secrets of men, according to my
gospel, by Jesus Christ. 'There are only two kinds of people in
the end', says C. S. Lewis: 'those who say to God "Thy will
be done" and those to whom God says in the end "Thy will be
done".'

D

CHAPTER FIVE

My Saviour

Jesus Christ, our Saviour (Titus 1⁴)
The Son of God, who loved me and gave himself up for
me (Gal 2²⁰)

IT IS one of the poignant facts of Christian history that men
have quarrelled about the exact way in which Jesus is to be
described as our Saviour. We have been puerile and silly at
the very point where we should have been most mature. It is
almost like a lover who does not want any photograph of his
sweetheart except from the one angle from which he himself
likes to view her. One tries not to be angry with those who
claim that they have a royal monopoly of the means whereby
Christ's grace reaches us. It is hard enough to bear the so-
called 'evangelicals' whose doctrine would suggest that we are
saved by a certain set of shibboleths and syllogisms. But there
are others who bring one to breaking-point, who call themselves Catholic (pronounced Carthòlic) and then go on to
make it clear that Christ's saviourhood is limited to those
standing in a certain confined circle.

Jesus is the Saviour of the world. This tremendous history-
determining factor is so vast a conception that no one of His
redeemed has ever said all that can be said about Him. What
matters is that we should understand Jesus to be our Saviour
in the ways that He Himself knew that He was our Saviour.
This means for instance that we have no right to say that He
is our deliverer from all pain, much as we may think that this
is a very comforting idea, for the simple reason that Christ
never promised this. Nor can we say that Jesus, as our
Saviour, delivers us from all ignorance—because there are
still many things He has to say to us, including the hour of His
return, and we cannot bear them yet. Nor can we say that He

rescues us from having to live as citizens and indeed as sub-
jects of Herod and Hitler. But Saviour He is, and Paul's
concern is to understand the meaning of redemption as
accomplished by the Redeemer Himself and not as a pre-
Christian Jew would have conceived of it. To come to the
point, did Paul think of the Saviour as the Saviour thought of
Himself?

This for many is the crux of the whole matter, and if Paul
fails at this point, the whole contention of our present study
is contradicted. 'Paulinism' is the disparaging term which is
used to suggest that Paul gave a new twist to the teaching and
work of Jesus, so that his was, in effect, a different religion.
'According to this view', says James Stewart, 'Paul was the
arch-corrupter of the Gospel. God sent His Son to be a
solution: Paul made Him a problem. Jesus bade men to consider the lilies and trust like little children; Paul spoke of
justifying faith. Jesus had a Cross; Paul had a doctrine of
atonement. Therefore, it is said, let us away from the Christ
of dogma to the Christ of history.'[1]

And yet, if one summarizes briefly the conception of Jesus
as Saviour found in His own words and (much more important)
in the implication of His actions, and if one then puts this
alongside the apostolic teaching as found in the Acts and the
epistles, one finds that the two pictures are in all essential points
identical.

Their main features are something like this: Jesus is the one
and only promised Messiah, born of the family of David. He
is God's own Son, sent in the flesh of man by the Father.
Though He had existed before time began, He is the new
beginning of the human race. He has a work of reconciliation
to accomplish. This He begins at the level of preaching the
Kingdom of God. The message is ratified by His deeds, as He
goes about doing good and healing all manner of diseases.
But the act of at-one-ment is only accomplished when, in His
own person, the sin of men and the grace of God come into
violent contact. The war between God and the spiritual

[1] *A Man in Christ*, p. 18.

hosts of wickedness reaches its once-for-all climax in the
Battle of the Passion. Jesus is a willing victim who is made a
triumphant victor by the mighty act of God in raising Him
from the dead. All that He does for men can be appropriated
by anyone, but on one condition alone, and that is the response
of faith to grace. Furthermore, all who accept His work on
their behalf must accept Christ Himself, and in accepting
Him they are identified with His dying and rising again in
a life of self-denying but victorious holiness through the
enabling power of God's Spirit.

Now I defy anyone to prove that this is not the picture of
Himself presented by Jesus to the world. This is also the
interpretation which Paul placed on the saving work of Christ.
No one of course will deny that Paul had his own theological
comments—call them elaborations if you will—but they are
the reflections of a man who worships the authentic Saviour of
mankind, and in no sense are they a statement of new doctrine.
If Paul censured those who taught anything different from his
own message, how much more would he have condemned his
own heart for teaching anything different from the Gospel of
Jesus Himself. He only wants us to learn of him as he has
learned of Christ. 'If any man teacheth a different doctrine,
and consenteth not to sound words, even the words of our
Lord Jesus Christ, . . . he is puffed up, knowing nothing, but
doting about questionings and disputes of words' (1 Tim 6³⁻⁴).
Paul is not going to be among those that 'trouble you and would
pervert the Gospel of Christ' (Gal 1⁷).

Let us now take the salient facts and see how Christ's mind
is faithfully represented by Paul.

(1) JESUS IS THE KEY TO SALVATION

This for some is a debatable statement, but certainly not for
either Jesus or Paul! Mankind's most common assertion is
that man is the key to his own salvation. The doctrine of self-
help is today as widespread as ever. It is far too prevalent in
the weekly (and weakly!) teaching of the Church. 'The root',
says John Ruskin, 'of almost every schism and heresy from

which the Christian Church has ever suffered has been the effort of man to earn rather than to receive his salvation.'

The greatest argument against the doctrine of self-help is that the very self with which we try to save ourselves is in need of salvation. A notable, if belated, awareness of this fact was seen in the life of C. E. M. Joad. After he had done untold damage to the spiritual convictions of a generation in need of sound doctrine, he wrote, in his prolix and turgid style: 'To me, the view of evil implied by Marxism, and expressed by Shaw and maintained by modern psychotherapy, a view which I adopted unthinkingly as a young man, which regards evil as the by-product of circumstances, which circumstances can therefore alter and even eliminate, has come to seem intolerably shallow, and the contrary view of it as endemic in man, more particularly in its Christian form, the doctrine of original sin, to express a deep and essential insight into human nature.'

Endemic or original sin rules out the possibility of self-help. 'Apart from me ye can do nothing' (Jn 15⁵), said Jesus unequivocally. 'Other foundation', says Paul, 'can no man lay than that which is laid, which is Jesus Christ' (1 Cor 3¹¹). According to Acts 9²⁷, immediately after his conversion Paul straight away, in the town of Damascus, set about 'proving that Jesus was the Christ'. There is no hint in Jesus or Paul that the world will ever have to look for another Saviour now that Jesus has come. (In passing, let us ask ourselves whether we as Christians give the impression to the world that this is an urgent fact from which no man can safely escape.)

God has dealt with an otherwise incurable situation. He has provided a bridge, and that bridge is Christ. We see the first disciples vaguely grasping this tremendous truth. When Peter said 'Thou art the Christ' he cannot possibly have known all the implications, but at least he saw in Jesus the one hope of a link between himself and God.

There is a scene in a story by Gerald Kerach where a partisan in Yugoslavia escaping from the Nazis is told by his leader that they must build a bridge. ' "We certainly must build a bridge," the partisan agreed, and added the comment: "You see, a voice at the back of my heart told me that when Klemen said that we had to build a bridge, he knew how to do it, and I was ready to follow him".' The Christian is one who knows 'at the back of his heart' that the one and only bridge-builder between God and men is Jesus Christ our Lord. He alone is able to reconcile.

(2) THE NECESSITY OF HIS DEATH

This bald phrase seems so obvious to any who have found life through Christ's death, that it is hard for us to grasp how shocking the thought must have been to the apostles. Apart from the scandal of crucifixion to a Jew, 'dead men tell no tales', and dead men have finished their work. Yet it was only by being a dead man that Jesus could in fact finish His work. He gave a repeated and loving warning to His apostles that the Son of Man must go and be crucified, but their ears and eyes were holden. Old Testament prophecy had given men a vision of a Servant whose life-giving was the giving of life, and Jesus fully and faithfully accepted this role laid upon Him by His Father: 'Thus it is written, that the Christ should suffer' (Lk 24[46]). Paul, as a Pharisee, had read and re-read the Scriptures, but it was only later that he knew for himself that Christ died for our sins, according to the Scriptures, and that He was raised on the third day, according to the Scriptures (1 Cor 15[3]).

There is a lovely story told about Lady Frederick Cavendish when she saw her uncle, Mr Gladstone, for the first time after the terrible news had come of her husband's murder in Phoenix Park. After a moment's silence, she said: 'Uncle William, you did right to send him to Ireland.' There came a time when the apostles knew that it had been right for the Father to send His Son to Jerusalem.

But Jesus had known it before it came to pass. It must not be imagined that Jesus went blindly through a dramatic part simply following the stage directions. It was His Father's will and way. That was all that mattered. His death had been

dimly foreseen by the prophets because they had dimly understood the nature of God's work, that through death comes life.
'A grain of wheat dies', says Jesus, 'in order that it may bear
fruit', which metaphor Paul picks up: 'that which thou thyself sowest' (he adds later that he is thinking of a grain of
wheat) 'is not quickened except it die' (1 Cor 15³⁶).

As well as this factor of life-from-death, we find that Paul
reaffirms the conviction of Jesus that it was necessary for Him
to undergo the whole impact of sin, even to the point of being
killed by it. In the phrase of the writer to the Hebrews: 'He
endured the gainsaying of sinners against Him.' If He had
endured less than death He would have failed to take the full
weight of men's resistance to God. He had 'to resist unto
blood, striving against sin'. 'Behoved it not the Christ to
suffer these things?' (Lk 24²⁶) said Jesus. So St Paul is found
in Thessalonica opening the Scriptures and 'alleging that it
behoved the Christ to suffer' (Acts 17³).

We are dealing summarily here with a theme which is
enough for a library of books. Sufficient to say that anyone
who dismisses the death of Jesus as being an unnecessary
accretion to His real work is robbing Jesus of His saviourhood
and Paul of his Saviour.

(3) THE DEATH OF JESUS WAS FOR ALL MEN

This is an unconditional statement; there are no 'ifs or buts',
especially for an Arminian. Christ died for all with no excep-
tions, most of all for the worst sinners. One can only *believe*
such a truth; one cannot understand it. With the greatest
stretch of charity possible to us, we cannot think of any life
being worth the life of Jesus. In fact in our moments of honest
judgement we can all think of men whose life does not seem
worth preserving at all. So it is worth noting straight away
that Jesus did not die so that all may go on existing as they are,
but that they may be saved for eternal life, which is a very
different matter.

One man died for the people, and the nearer He came to
His death, the more Jesus appears to have thought in terms of

the world. Dr Russell Maltby says that in the later stages of
Christ's ministry, 'every passing event stood in its true context of the eternal. No preoccupation with the present ob-
scured the history of the past or hid the significance of the
future: He was concerned with the whole. His help for each
individual was as prompt and kind as ever, but each individual
man was now EVERYMAN, a kind of representative; all his tribe
were speaking and acting in him. When the authorities were
taking counsel to make away with Him, now knowing what they
did, Jesus saw what they were doing and recognized it for what
it was. It was only what their fathers had said and done
before them. This was what men were; this was what they
were to be saved from. A long chapter in human history
was drawing to a close; He was there to wind it up and to open
the new. The "stage" was now "all the world", and the
players were "all the men and women" in it. The burden of
Christ was nothing less than the need of the world.'[1]

The whole of mankind, indeed the whole cosmos, was involved at the Cross, when, as the earth did quake and the rocks
were rent, Christ broke through the sin barrier.

It is the 'whosoever' of Jesus perhaps more than any other
word that has made us all feel encompassed by the arms of
love upon the Cross. In John 3[16], owing to the absence of
punctuation in Greek writing between verses 15 and 16, we
cannot be sure whether it was Jesus or John who said 'Whosoever believeth . . . ' and the Revised Version is non-committal
by starting a new paragraph at that point. But it is most
certainly the whole spirit of His offer to mankind that whosoever will may come. Here is what one of the saints of the
Church says: 'If the verse had read: "There is mercy for
Richard Baxter" or "God so loved Richard Baxter", I am so
vile, so sinful, that I would have thought it must have meant
some other Richard Baxter. But these words "the world" and
"whosoever" include the worst of Richard Baxters that ever
lived.'

Nothing is more certain in all the writings of Paul than that

[1] *Christ and His Cross*, p. 50.

he was convinced that Christ died for all: 'The grace of God, and the gift by the grace of the one man, Jesus Christ, abound unto the many' (Rom 5[15]); 'through the obedience of the one shall the many be made righteous' (Rom 5[19]); 'he died for all' (2 Cor 5[15]). When we are accused of making sweeping statements we can take comfort by looking at the New Testament references to '*all*' and seeing that we are in good company. Charles Wesley struck a blow against the wrong slant put on Calvin by many writers when he constantly reiterated the theme: 'For all, for all my Saviour died.'

What other so-called saviour of mankind has even in his most idealist moments thought of his work as being for every creature? All other 'redeemers' have breathed out warnings and threatenings to their enemies; no other 'saviour' has stretched his arms so wide. When Arthur Hopkins, as a young Methodist Missionary in the West Indies, had been for the first time celebrating Holy Communion at a Home of Refuge for paupers, he wrote: 'As I dispensed the elements, giving them into those poor folk's hands, I felt a great joy. For indeed His blood was shed for them. I don't think anyone else would consent to die for them, but *He* did. As I placed the bread in their black hands, and gave them the wine, I felt a wave of gladness come over me.'

When reason has done its utmost to complicate matters, the moment of reality can come to any soul who sees Christ on His Cross, and who says with Paul in faith: 'He loved me and gave Himself up for me.'

(4) CHRIST WAS ATTESTED AS SAVIOUR BY HIS RESURRECTION

We cannot but see the Cross through the sparkling light of Easter morning. That is why we are always right to make our Good Friday services a time of glory as well as of shame. His dying was mankind's finest hour. Stopford Brooke wrote to a friend on Good Friday: 'I ought to have gone to Church, but I did not go. I cannot stand the elaborate mourning which is practised in all the Churches for the most triumphant act of pure love which ever was done in the history of the world.'

But we rejoice at Calvary not only because it was an act of pure love, but far, far more because *it was not the end of the story.* (Neither for that matter was the Resurrection, for to leave the story unfinished before the Ascension, as so many do, is like walking out before the last act of a drama.) The Resurrection was the great act of vindication for Christ. By faith (and one must stress that Christ's true manhood demanded that it should be by faith alone) He went to His Cross trusting His Father to raise Him up on the third day. How dark was the night in which He held on to that faith no other soul can know.

> *I have a faint cold fear thrills through my veins,*
> *That almost freezes up the heat of life . . .*
> *My dismal scene I needs must act alone.*

Here again, it would be folly to suggest that Paul was in any sense in divergence from his Master in giving the Resurrection a supreme place in the scheme of salvation. 'He was delivered up for our trespasses, and was raised for our justification' (Rom 4[25]). Was not Paul constantly in trouble for 'preaching the Resurrection' (Acts 13[33, 37])? At Antioch he said: 'God raised Him from the dead'; 'He whom God raised up saw no corruption'. Before Agrippa, Festus speaks of 'one Jesus, who was dead, whom Paul affirmed to be alive' (Acts 25[19]). The living Saviour had His credentials in His own wounded hands. Paul died for this assertion. In a variety of ways, Paul tells the world that Jesus rose: 'Jesus was raised'; 'God raised Jesus'.

(5) JESUS SAVES ALL WHO HAVE FAITH

It is the doctrine of salvation by faith in the writings of Paul which has been a bugbear to some. But how can we say that this is in any way at variance with Christ's insistence that men should trust Him? How often Jesus 'saved' or 'healed' men in response to faith, and how often this whole process was dammed up by unbelief. It was as though Jesus had said: 'You can be put right if only you will have faith.' He asked for nothing but faith. Let me say that again—it was only faith He asked for. What is this but another way of saying that we are saved by faith alone?

Men will insist on doing a bit of their own salvation— paying a penance, working their passage part way. I love the story of the old lady with a heavy shopping-basket who was given a lift in a car. As she held her burden on her knee, the driver said: 'My dear, why don't you put your basket on the back seat?' 'No thank you, young man,' she said. 'If you are good enough to give me a lift, the least I can do is to carry my own basket.'

By grace are we saved, through faith, and there is nothing —at the point of our receiving salvation—that we are meant to do of ourselves. It is not intended that we should boast even of carrying part of the burden of our own redemption. It is all of grace. Here is the Protestant, Reformation—and Methodist—emphasis. 'Thy faith hath saved thee' (Lk 7^{50}), says Jesus. 'By grace have ye been saved', says Paul, 'through faith; and that not of yourselves: it is the gift of God' (Eph 2^8). The Gospel is 'the power of God unto salvation to every one that *believeth*' (Rom 1^{16}).

(6) CHRIST'S WORK IS REPRODUCED IN THE SAVED

It is Christ who saves, not His Cross. It is a person, not place or postulates. No intermediary, no sacred relics are needed. When a college friend of Oliver Cromwell asked him as a favour that a silver cross in the church where he was vicar should be preserved from the spoiling hands of Roundhead soldiers, Cromwell said that this request was granted provided that he was going to engrave on the back the words: 'Worship Christ not the Cross.'

I have never been entirely happy in my own mind when people speak about clinging to the 'Old Rugged Cross'. One feels far happier saying with Paul: 'Who shall separate us from the love of Christ?' He asks that question just after he has been talking about the Christ who also maketh intercession for us. It is Christ, our Intercessor, to whom we cling. I sometimes feel myself holding on to Christ as a man under judgement in the courts will hover around the advocate who is pleading his case.

A coloured girl wrote to a minister friend of mine: 'Please pray for me. Please don't think that I don't pray for myself, I do, but I would like you to speak to God for me because you know how to speak to Him better than I do. Please thank him for all that He has done for me.' If you know yourself to be under the judgement of God, there is hope for you and you will be saved in that hope, if you keep very close to Christ, who alone is fit to speak to God on our behalf.

> *What shall I say Thy grace to move?*
> *Lord, I am sin, but Thou art Love;*
> *I give up every plea beside,*
> *'Lord, I am damned, but Thou hast died.'*

Christ crucified, risen and ascended is able to save only in so far as we receive *him* and allow the whole process of death and new birth to come to pass in us. Dr R. W. Dale said: 'God does not redeem us merely by revealing His love; He reveals His love by redeeming us.' Many inadequate doctrines of the Cross are proclaimed and most of them err through belittling Christ's achievement and stopping short of His full salvation. The man who accepts the saving work of Christ is thereby 'saved', but he is also 'beginning to be saved' and is furthermore making ready one day 'to be fully saved'. The past is behind him. His sins are forgiven for Jesus's sake. But the work goes on just in so far as he is becoming a new creature. A man in a radio play whose wife had been unfaithful to him but had returned, in penitence, said of her: 'It is not what 'er 'as been as matters, it's what 'er is.' So the Christian is one who lives for Him who died for all, or he is no Christian in the full sense of the term. Christ 'died for all, that they which live should no longer live unto themselves, but unto him who for their sakes died and rose again' (2 Cor 5[15]).

In his own way, Paul approached the words of Christ which we find in the fourth gospel; Christ has not completed His work as Saviour until He abides in us and we in Him. Yet no phrase or illustration or anecdote can fully portray this truth. Jesus speaks of our being in the Vine, which is Christ. Paul speaks of our being in the Body, which is Christ. The implication is the same, that He is Saviour to the uttermost when we are utterly His possession. This involves dying and rising again, enduring the Cross and living victoriously. 'We are more than conquerors through him that loved us' (Rom 8[37]) and goes on loving us.

CHAPTER SIX

My Kinsmen

My kinsmen according to the flesh:
who are Israelites (Rom 9³)

A STRONG CASE could be made for the assertion that the life of St Paul is one of the greatest examples of turn-coat treachery in the history of the human race. Those who are for and those who are against Christ—this is the most significant division of humanity, and according to Jesus it is of eternal significance which side you are on. St Paul changes from one side to the other. He is not merely a convert from the ranks of the neutrals. From being public prosecutor No. 1, inveighing against Jesus as Public Enemy No. 1, he swings over to join the advance guard of Christ's followers. The Christ he has persecuted has now become his master, with the result that those he has put in prison become his fellow prisoners.

But this is the very measure of his conversion. Paul was an all-or-nothing man. There are no propagandists, whether it be in religion, or politics, or the arts, more fanatical and rabid than those who have completely changed their minds. The psychological cynic may say that all this is due to a man's desire to justify his apostasy and save his face. But just as often it is because a man is trying to tell as many as possible that he now admits that he has been calling darkness light, and light darkness, and that he must make up for lost time.

This was the situation with St Paul. The irony of it did not escape him, but he had one consuming loyalty—his new master and Saviour. Christ is always our cure for the tensions of life. If we fear Him, we have nothing else to fear. If He matters most to us, nothing else much matters. After life-long frustration and temporary total blindness, Paul's eyes were opened to see the King of the Jews, his compatriot and kinsman. From then on, he took over his master's mind, and this decided his attitude and his actions in relation to his own Jewish background.

If we say: 'What is the relevance of all this to a modern Christian? I am not a Jew concerned with the treatment of fellow Jews,' the answer is that each one of us in our own way has a responsibility to 'our own folk'. Jesus warned us that a man's worst enemies might well be of his own household, and this is a particularly pressing problem with some who are the first to be followers in their own home. One cannot release such people from responsibility towards their kinsmen by saying 'Perhaps you are not the most suitable one to help them'. Evangelism begins at home, and in many instances Christian discipleship involves a great deal of 'speaking the truth in love' to those who are embarrassingly near to us.

Let us watch how St Paul follows his master, stage by stage, through a logical scheme of thought. Far from betraying his own compatriots, he is only following in the steps of Him for whose coming Abraham and the Fathers had prepared the way.

To begin with, they were his own people, his brethren. Probably few of us can enter fully into the sense of patriotic pride experienced by a Pharisee of the Pharisees. A Scot, a Welsh-Nationalist, a pure Aryan German—these are but pale reflections of the typical Jew to whom his race was a divine trusteeship. Paul never disowned this blood tie any more than Jesus did. Not even citizenship of Tarsus could compare with his boast that 'I am a Jew of the tribe of Abraham'. As surely as Jesus would rejoice to hear the children of Jerusalem crying: 'Hosanna to the Son of David', so St Paul would relish the taunt made at Philippi: 'These men, being Jews, do exceedingly trouble our city' (Acts 16[20]).

Even as a Christian, he is still ready to be a Jew to Jews, in the hope of saving some. Christ weeps over His kinsmen of Jerusalem (Lk 19[41]), and Paul's heart's desire and supplication is that his people should be saved (Rom 10[1]). No wonder that among all his administrations in a fresh territory, he is often found first going to his own people to win them for the Messiah. If we compare the concordance references in St John's Gospel and in the Acts to the word 'Jew', we shall see how similar to that of Jesus is Paul's devotion to the Jews, as well as his treatment at their hands. A typical instance of this is at Thessalonica, when in the synagogue he reasoned with them. 'This Jesus, whom, said he, I proclaim unto you, is the Christ. And some of them were persuaded. . . . But the Jews, being moved with jealousy, took unto them certain vile fellows of the rabble, and gathering a crowd, set the city on an uproar' (Acts 17^{3-5}).

Far from seeking to alienate them, he does all in his power to win their confidence. Had not his master paid the temple tax? Shall Paul not risk apparent compromise by consenting to the circumcision of Timothy, son of Greek and Jewish parents? Jesus had come to His own home and been rejected by His own people; Paul is ready to be accursed even from Christ for his brethren's sake. Although he had been a persecutor of the Christians, when he joined their ranks he never became a persecutor of Jews, but rather in the spirit of his master, prayed for them that despitefully used him.

Neither Paul nor Jesus ever questioned Israel's priority in the plans of God. It was a case of 'To the Jew first . . .'. The lost people of the tribe of Israel were precious because they belonged to a very special flock. But the nature of Israel's privilege was that they were called to be the servant of God and that involved a calling to vicarious suffering. The people of God had been saved to serve, not to be the pampered darlings of history. It is here that we see their great failure to fulfil the purposes of God.

Israel had been given three tasks of consummate importance and in all these she had failed; if Paul is honest about this, he is only following the lead of Jesus Himself.

(A) ISRAEL WAS THE GUARDIAN OF THE LAW

The word 'law' has about it a stern intimidating note. When we view it in the wrong light, it has the appearance of a giant thwarting our path to freedom; it seems an intrusive spoil-sport like an inhibiting mother who says: 'Find out what Jimmy is doing and tell him not to!' In English life we have our own disparaging phrases to show our impatience with authority. We speak, and in an ungrateful tone, about 'rules and regulations'. We say that we abhor red-tape, though it may help to bind up the wounds of society. We emphasize the negative aspect of law, and say that we do not like all these 'Thou-shalt-nots'. Far too readily we look on the ruler, the magistrate, the policeman, as men to be feared and certainly to be avoided. All this, of course, applies only when we see the law in relation to the curtailment of our liberties. It is a very different matter when we are considering our rights, and the defence of our homes and possessions. Then we see the law as a glorious and chivalrous St George, whom we call in to save us from life's dragons.

To the Jews, the Law was a bequest from God, and, above all, the gift of His love. Moses had received a priceless treasure over which Israel was to keep watch and guard for all time. The Law was no ugly intrusion, but the very hem of God's garment. It has been said that to the rabbinic Jew the Law was both an institution and a faith. 'Thy statutes are my song' sang the Psalmist. The words of the Lord (which included above all the Law) were 'more to be desired than pure gold' (Ps 19[10]). This was why a Jewish child on his first day at school was sometimes given a slate covered with honey. When the child licked off the honey, there could be seen written on the slate: 'How sweet are Thy words unto my taste! Yea, sweeter than honey to my mouth!' (Ps 119[103]). It was for love's sake that Israel had been warned against murder and stealing and false witness and covetousness. Who would dream of calling it any more than a loving act, when a father tells his child not to poke the electric-light point with a pair of scissors. He is telling the child not to do something he wants to do; but, far more important, he is telling the child not to do something he will regret having done.

The oracles of God, says Paul, have been entrusted to Israel,

E

whose are 'the covenants, and the giving of the Law, . . . and the promises' (Rom 9⁴). 'Salvation is from the Jews' (Jn 4²²), says Jesus, referring not only to His own coming but to the precious guide to holy living in the Law. Jesus makes constant allusions to Moses' having given them the Law from God. The Law in itself was a blessing not a curse. The Law was in a sense the only mediator men had before the coming of Christ. 'The law was given by Moses; grace and truth came by Jesus Christ' (Jn 1¹⁷); but both gifts were given by the Lord God. The Law, says Paul, was our tutor to lead us to Christ (Gal 3²⁴). By this he probably meant that it was like the child's first governess who took the child to school. It was a preparation for full salvation in the School of Charity. But nothing about the Law would need to be unlearnt or cancelled. 'Till heaven and earth pass away, one jot or one tittle shall in no wise pass away from the law.' But Israel has failed in the use she made of this unique treasure, and Paul knows this from painful personal experience.

(1) *First they had increasingly become slaves under a yoke rather than sons loving their Father's will*

The spirit of bondage marked the character and life of the Pharisee. It is sometimes claimed that Jesus was unfair to Pharisees, and that He was harsh with men who had a sensitive conscience and who in days of liberty were upholding the standards of morality. But who is ever wrong to be angry about slavery? If a son is living in servile thraldom to his father, and dragging his brothers down into the same pit, is it wrong to long for him to know instead what it is to be a son bound to his father's will only with filial fear and loving respect?

Paul saw in his own life the very tragedy which Jesus diagnosed in the Pharisees. Duty, not love, had become his relationship with God. Then the grace of our Lord Jesus Christ had entered in to enable him to fulfil the Law's demands in a way that he had never been able to fulfil them, even as a conscientious slave.

(2) *In the second place, Israel had failed to handle the Law aright because through the centuries there had been added man-made accretions of petty ordinances*

It helps us to understand some of the anger of Jesus with the Pharisees if we realize that He was revolted by the sight of something fine and beautiful being messed about by the addition of finicky trifles. One can imagine standing with John Betjeman in a beautiful building that has been ruined by amateur 'improvements' and hearing his comments—'The original was magnificent, integral and honest, but see what fiddlers have made of it.'

To Jesus the Law had towered above human life as His Father's good and acceptable and perfect will for men, but to this loving purpose men had added their own footnotes and addenda. The Sabbath had been the glorious contribution to men's well-being. The Scribes and Pharisees had made it look like a silly set of bye-laws for an LCC cab-rank. Jesus never broke the Law of the Sabbath which His Father had, in love, ordained; what He broke was the *periphery* of regulations which had accumulated through the years. Rules of health and hygiene which were intended as a guide for men wanting to live to the glory of God had become a collection of minute injunctions probing into peccadilloes so that men had to walk warily all their days. In many cases instructions designed for a nomadic people living in tents had been preserved, elaborated and fossilized long after the need for them had disappeared.

Paul's eyes were opened to all this when he discovered that there was now no condemnation for them that were in Christ Jesus, but instead the glorious liberty of a son of God. His kinsmen had been misled, and he with them. Peter had talked about 'a yoke upon the neck of the disciples, which neither our fathers nor we were able to bear' (Acts 15[10]).

So, says St Paul to the Galatians: 'With freedom did Christ set us free; stand fast therefore, and be not entangled again in a yoke of bondage' (Gal 5[1]). Jesus Christ had opened Paul's eyes when He had said to the multitudes and to His disciples:

'The Scribes and the Pharisees sit on Moses' seat; all things therefore whatsoever they bid you, these do and observe' (that is, when they teach what Moses taught); 'But do not ye after their works; they bind heavy burdens and grievous to be borne and lay them on men's shoulders' (Mt 23[1-4]). So, says St Paul, 'Israel, following after a law of righteousness, did not arrive at that law. Wherefore? Because they sought it not by faith, but as it were by works' (Rom 9[31-2]). Their failure meant that they had lost the very Law which was entrusted to them.

(B) ISRAEL WAS HOST TO THE MESSIAH

It may not always be easy for us to be as confident as the authors of the gospels and the epistles in the quotations they use from the Old Testament to 'prove' the fact that Israel had anticipated the Messiah. (It is not always easy to see the relevance of a quotation in a modern preacher's sermon!) To us many of the references used by Matthew, for instance, seem rabbinic and far-fetched, but one thing is certain—that Israel lived in hope, and this hope was focused on the Coming One, and the Coming One was to be 'of the seed of David', and the day when He should arrive would be a day that could best be described as a day of good news. It would be a day of the King, the Mediator and the once-for-all Sacrifice.

We make havoc of the gospel narrative if we fail to see that Jesus knew himself to be the Coming One. He had come to His own home, and His own people were not receiving Him. At His baptism, at His transfiguration, at Caesarea Philippi, at His passion and after His resurrection, He accepted it as a fact that Israel had received and was rejecting the One for whom they had been longing. So we are not surprised that Paul, with the authority of Christ Himself, said he was unashamed of this gospel (Rom 1[16]).

The Saviour had come, and been, and gone, and come again. The power of God for salvation was now released in the world. All that Jesus had said of Himself in relation to the Law and the Prophets and the Writings as the hope and consolation of Israel Paul knew to be true to fact.

But the Jews had failed utterly, tragically, and, save for repentance, unforgivably. In two ways, Paul shared Christ's judgement on their kinsmen:

(1) *They had been blinded by unbelief*

The prophets had been well aware of this terrible phenomenon in human life: that men lose the very powers of apprehension which God has given them, and that through their own grievous fault. How are we to understand all this talk about hearing and deliberately misunderstanding and having eyes and stubbornly not seeing? Perhaps we can catch a glimpse of it as we think of a child, headstrong and wayward, determined to have his own way. Can you argue? Can you reason? No, he will work himself up into such a tantrum that he will call black white, and white black, until you throw up your hands in adult despair and say: 'I can't get any sense out of him.' Jesus quoted Isaiah: 'He hath blinded their eyes, and he hardened their heart' (Jn 12[40]). The worst had happened and God had let it happen. They had hardened their hearts; their hearts had been hardened; God had hardened their hearts. The terrible pattern of Pharaoh's sin had been repeated. Nazareth had rejected the prophet in His own country, and Jesus marvelled at their unbelief. The Jews had asked for signs, and yet no sign, not even the sign of Jonah, is of any avail with men who shut their eyes, and seal their ears. There are none so blind as those that will not see. It is this horrific picture which Paul portrayed when he exposed his kinsmen to themselves. He, too, quoted Isaiah 6: 'This people's heart is waxed gross and their ears are dull of hearing and their eyes they have closed' (Acts 28[27]). He said to the Romans: 'That which Israel seeketh for, that he obtained not' (Rom 11[7]).

(2) *The Jews were no better than their fathers in their treatment of God's Messenger*

The treatment of the prophets should make us think hard in these days when it is a rare thing for a preacher to be shouted down. It might be good for those of us who are preachers to check the warm glow that comes over us when in the porch we are thanked for 'a nice sermon', and to ask ourselves if it might not have been the sign of a better sermon if we had received a ripe tomato on the forehead. You cannot make yourself a prophet by saying objectionable things, but if you are a true prophet, you will probably be objectionable. People will 'take exception' to what you say. Did not the Master say that a 'local' preacher was not 'acceptable'! (Lk 4²⁴).

The prophets had been the daily reading of Jesus through His youth and He knew only too well how they had been treated. The Temptation was in part a phase of this inevitable rejection. When He addressed the Pharisees He scorned the smugness with which they imagined that if they had been on the scene at the time of a martyrdom, they would have been the defenders of righteousness. 'Woe unto you . . . for ye . . . say, If we had been in the days of our fathers, we should not have been partakers with them in the blood of the prophets. Wherefore ye witness to yourselves, that ye are sons of them that slew the prophets. Fill ye up the measure of your fathers' (Mt 23²⁹⁻³²). 'O Jerusalem, Jerusalem, which killeth the prophets, and stoneth them that are sent unto her' (Mt 23³⁷). 'The blood of all the prophets may be required of this generation' (Lk 11⁵⁰). 'If they hear not Moses and the prophets, neither will they be persuaded, if one rise from the dead' (Lk 16³¹). The parable of the Wicked Husbandmen linked the tragedy of Israel's treatment of the prophets with the final scene of the killing of the Owner's Son.

This charge was taken up by the apostles from the very first days, one might say the very first hours, of the early Church. Said Peter at Pentecost: 'Let all the house of Israel therefore know assuredly, that God hath made Him both Lord and Christ, this Jesus whom ye crucified' (Acts 2³⁶). And Stephen at his defence made the same accusation: 'Which of the prophets did not your fathers persecute? and they killed them which shewed before of the coming of the Righteous

One; of whom ye have now become betrayers and murderers' (Acts 7[52]). Paul takes up the plaint and speaks of the Jews who 'both killed the Lord Jesus and the prophets, and drave out us' (1 Thess 2[15]). It was all of a piece; God's people would not receive God's messengers.

(c) ISRAEL WAS GOD'S AMBASSADOR TO THE WORLD

That the Church must proclaim God's message to the world is a truism to the Christian, but to the Jew the duty of winning the world for the Lord Jehovah was by no means so obvious. Even a Christian Church may put up posters proclaiming the Kingdom Overseas and then leave them unread until they hang in tatters, and although the Jew had been told by the prophets about the task to which he was called, he paid little attention. It is one thing to hear a statement of the truth and quite another to live by its implications. We can be sure that Jesus lived all His days in the consciousness of the promise that in Abraham and his seed all the families of the earth would be blessed. Jesus would not have forgotten His reading of second Isaiah—Israel had been 'called in righteousness . . . for a light of the Gentiles' (Isa 42[6]); 'I will give thee for a light to the Gentiles, that thou mayest be my salvation unto the end of the earth' (Isa 49[6]); 'all the ends of the earth shall see the salvation of our God' (Isa 52[10]). Jesus had no less a vision of the world redeemed than had the aged Simeon who held Him as an infant in arms, as a 'light for revelation to the Gentiles'.

It cannot be denied that Jesus saw His first mission to be to the lost sheep of the tribe of Israel. But if He seemed to show some reluctance to turn aside from His one increasing purpose in order to help a Syrophoenician woman, this is only to be interpreted as a measure of His love for Israel. The implications of world evangelization are embedded in His teaching. The story of the Good Samaritan was not only a lesson in common kindness; it was even more an eye-opener concerning the nature of a man's neighbourhood. 'Jews have no dealings with Samaritans' was a slogan answered by Jesus

even as He talked to the woman who quoted it. But Israel
had failed to retain a sense of the limitless promises of God to
Abraham. 'All the families', 'All the nations of the earth'—
these are strong unequivocal phrases, but they bear little
likeness to the narrow attitude of the Judaism of Christ's day.

> O that the chosen band
>   Might now their brethren bring,
> And, gathered out of every land,
>   Present to Zion's King!
> Of all the ancient race
>   Not one be left behind,
> But each, impelled by secret grace,
>   His way to Canaan find.

(1) *They had monopolized the title of 'Sons of Abraham'*

John the Baptist had done his best; he had scorned their
self-satisfied sense of security. 'Think not to say within yourselves, We have Abraham to our father: for I say unto you,
that God is able of these stones to raise up children unto
Abraham' (Mt 3⁹). Jesus spoke even more strongly to such
people and told them that they had the Devil, and not
Abraham, as their father (Jn 8⁴⁴).

Even though it always surprises us to think of Jesus being
taken by surprise, the fact remains that He was amazed at the
belief in the Gentile centurion. It was as a guide for the next
urgent campaign that He told His twelve apostles: 'Go not
into any way of the Gentiles, and enter not into any city of the
Samaritans' (Mt 10⁵). His own practice was different—a
friend of sinners did not come into the world as a patron of the
policy of exclusive Judaism. He visited the 'Galilee of the
Gentiles' (Mt 4¹⁵), and He pondered over Tyre and Sidon, and
He 'taught those who sought Him from Decapolis'. The grate-
ful leper was a Samaritan. Jesus said that the men of Nineveh
and the Queen of Sheba would one day rise up in judgement
against that generation. Even when the Pharisees did show
any sign of missionary zeal, it was to compass sea and land

only to make a man two-fold more the son of hell than themselves (Mt 23¹⁵).

Now St Paul stands up in history as a true son of Abraham, committed to Christ's service and with a gospel for all the world, Jew and Gentile. Like John the Baptist, he scorned their confidence in their own racial security. They had not exactly made a success of things. 'If thou bearest the name of a Jew, and restest upon the law . . . thou therefore that teachest another, teachest thou not thyself?' (Rom 2¹⁷⁻²¹). 'He is not a Jew which is one outwardly, but he is a Jew which is one inwardly.' There is no monopoly in the realm of God's salvation. 'They are not all Israel which are of Israel, neither because they are Abraham's seed are they all children.' 'In Christ Jesus neither circumcision availeth nor uncircumcision, but faith working through love.' Most of the Epistle to the Galatians is devoted to this theme. The promise by faith in Jesus Christ is given to them that believe. 'If ye are Christ's then are ye Abraham's seed—heirs according to promise.' He sums it up in one of the greatest missionary texts in the Bible: 'Christ hath been made a minister of the circumcision for the truth of God, that He might confirm the promises given unto the fathers, and that the Gentiles might glorify God for His mercy' (Rom 15⁸⁻⁹).

(2) *Their life had been turned in on themselves*

We catch a glimpse in some of the parables of the indignation of Jesus against the selfishness of the Jews. Dives is condemned for simply not bothering about the poor man at his gate; the elder brother has no concern about the restoration of the prodigal. Montefiore reminded us that the emphasis in the life of Jesus on going out to seek and save the lost was something quite new to Judaism. Their's was the sin of self-containedness, the sin that is condemned in the 'in-as-much-as-ye-did-it-not' judgement of Christ.

Of the promises of God, Israel had said 'these are ours to hold', not 'these are ours to share'. The selfish man is not worried so long as he is all right, but why is it that God cannot sleep? It is because He is counting sheep!—97, 98, 99 . . . and so long as there is one still to be gathered in, His heart yearns.

Paul's missionary zeal was fired by the Spirit of Christ that will not let us rest in happy fellowship, content that we are among those that have the gospel and need not worry about those that have not. It is a wonderful sign of conversion that Paul, whose whole upbringing . . . had led him to think 'I was glad when they said unto me, Let us go into the house of the Lord. . . . Pray for the peace of Jerusalem', could say: 'After I have been to Jerusalem I must also see Rome.'

This three-fold failure as guardian of the Law, as host to Christ, as ambassador to the Gentiles, meant that Israel had lost her chance. She was to be supplanted. The whole stream of God's grace has now broken the banks of the river; it is flowing on into history. There is now a New Israel in being, a new Building is being erected and the very stone which Israel has rejected has been made Head of the corner.

> *Lord over all, if thou hast made,*
> *Hast ransomed every soul of man,*
> *Why is the grace so long delayed?*
> *Why unfulfilled the saving plan?*
> *The bliss, for Adam's race designed,*
> *When will it reach to all mankind?*
>
> *Art thou the God of Jews alone?*
> *And not the God of Gentiles too?*
> *To Gentiles make thy goodness known;*
> *Thy judgements to the nations show;*
> *Awake them by the gospel call;*
> *Light of the world, illumine all!*

CHAPTER SEVEN

My Beloved in the Lord

Salute Ampliatus my beloved in the Lord (Rom 16⁸)

WE HAVE seen that Paul was truly in line with his master in
breaking through the confines of the old Israel. The Vineyard
was now going to have an extended hedge, and all who are in
Christ are within the New Israel.

There is a deep concern in these days about the doctrine
of the Church. With many it is an all-embracing obsession,
almost to the exclusion of concern about the doctrine of
Christ and His atonement. It is hard to be patient sometimes
with those who seem to put His Church before Christ. I
remember hearing John Huxtable say that if the Church is all
that some people say it is, he could not understand why some
people did not actually worship it. Perhaps they do! But this
introversive concentration on the new Israel is as dangerous
as that on the old Israel. There is a self-consciousness about
it which is not altogether healthy. It is possible for a family
to be so clan-conscious that their behaviour is reminiscent of
a secret society in the school playground.

Nowadays there are many analyses of the Church, many
definitions, and many grandiloquent phrases. The Church is
this; the Church is that—men still search for a formula to
define its exact confines. 'Where the Bishop is, there is the
Church'; 'Where the Bible is (provided you interpret it as we
do), there is the Church'; 'Where the Table is, there is the
Church'; 'Where the denominational statement of faith is,
there is the Church'; and so on and on. My own guess is that
if we are honest, we probably all feel that we give the Church
exactly the right place in the scheme of Christian theology.
In the words of the shaving-soap advertisement: 'Not too
little, not too much, but just right!' When we all get to

Heaven, we shall be forced to laugh at ourselves and see all our denominational enclosures as nothing more than man-made hedges to keep recalcitrant sheep within some sort of a fold.

But however much we ourselves may err in interpretation, by overstating or underestimating the significance of the Church, one thing is certain, that for both Jesus and Paul the Church was of supreme importance. It was not a convenient little society founded to keep the movement going. 'Christ loved the church and gave himself up for it' (Eph 5²⁵). The Church is part of the cosmic plan of salvation and we are always right to say: 'Outside the Church there is no salvation' (for one obvious reason—that if you are 'saved' you are already inside). What Christian can be so vulgar as to speak disparagingly of the Bride of Christ?

Our immediate concern is to ask: 'Did Paul catch Christ's mind in relation to the Church?' It will not surprise us that Paul, perhaps here less than anywhere, does not quote any actual words of Jesus, since the word 'Church' is scarcely on the Master's lips, but we shall find once again that Paul is full of Christ's Spirit and in line with His teaching. He does not miss his way in this important sphere of belief.

The picture that we get of the Church from both Jesus and St Paul is in essence a quite simple story of the unfolding purpose of God's love, as men are gathered by grace, through faith, into that company which Paul calls 'My beloved in the Lord'. For instance, we could say that a picture of the Church is to be seen in the vignette at the end of St John's Gospel. 'Jesus saith unto Simon: Lovest thou me? Peter saith: Lord, thou knowest all things; thou knowest that I love thee. Jesus saith: Feed my sheep' (Jn 21¹⁷). In a similar way, the simple rudiments of the Church are in that scene where St Paul says farewell at Miletus to his friends from Ephesus: speaking of the ministry which he received from the Lord Jesus to testify the gospel and the grace of God he says: 'Take heed unto yourselves, and to all the flock ... and they all wept sore, and fell on Paul's neck, and kissed him' (Acts 20²⁸, ³⁷).

But there are other grander things to be said about the Church of God. Jesus has His mystic imagery concerning the future of the Church 'to which shall be gathered the tribes of all the earth, coming from the north and the south and the east and the west', to sit down at the Messianic Banquet. So St Paul in a symphony of words without music, speaks in majestic phrases in Ephesians, chapters 1–3, and it is almost as though he cannot stop as he tells of the historic and cosmic purposes of God yet to be worked out through the Church.

Now we shall see the unity of Paul's mind with that of Christ if we examine briefly some of the crisp phrases which are in themselves descriptive of the Church's origin and function.

(1) 'REPENT AND BELIEVE IN THE GOSPEL'

The Church is a company of converts. No one ought to be too dogmatic as to when the Church came into being. Some would say it was with the call of Abraham; others, with St Mark, 'the beginning of the Gospel—John came'. Others again would pinpoint Caesarea Philippi and Peter's declaration of faith. Or again, one could say that the Church's story began at the Ascension, or that she was born at Pentecost.

There is much, however, to be said for the view that the Church of Christ as we know it began to exist at the time when Jesus came into Galilee, preaching 'Repent and believe in the Gospel'. This marked the beginning of the divine offer of salvation through Christ, and whoever closes with this offer in repentance and faith is within the Church. The glory of the Gospel is that Christ came *giving* repentance and not only demanding it. Samuel Taylor Coleridge said: 'The supreme promise of the Gospel is not forgiveness to those who repent, but repentance to those who sin.' True churchmanship is based on a simple act of penitence and faith. That is why it is no bad thing to begin each Sunday's worship by saying: 'I will arise and go to my father, and will say unto him, Father, I have sinned.' This is where Jesus begins with us all.

There must be a conscious turn-about of ourselves to Him, a deliberate break with our past, and this break is simply and dramatically represented in our baptism.

St Paul's first task as a preacher of his new-found Gospel, as he tells King Agrippa, was to declare 'both to them of Damascus first, and at Jerusalem . . . that they should repent and turn to God, doing works worthy of repentance' (Acts 26[20]). It was his primary task to testify both to Jews and to Greeks 'repentance toward God, and faith toward our Lord Jesus Christ' (Acts 20[21]). We should never fail to make it clear that the first condition of membership is penitence, a sincere desire to be saved from our sins through faith in Jesus Christ. This would deter us from filling up our churches with people who feel rather pleased with themselves for having decided to patronize a struggling institution.

(2) 'COME WITH ME'

The Church is the Society of the Friends of Jesus. It would be no uncommon sight in Palestine for people to see a travelling preacher followed by a crocodile of admiring disciples. No one but Jesus knew that He and those who accompanied Him were of an entirely different order from anything that had been seen before. This was the Church in embryo. That expressive phrase 'the gathered Church' speaks of the elemental fact that Jesus plus two people constitute a Church. It was a revolutionary concept that two or three gathered together could form a quorum for devotion.

A friend of mine used to have his church hall used by a Jewish congregation. It quite often happened that a service would have to be delayed while someone ran down the road to various homes in order to get one or two members to make up the requisite quorum of ten worshippers before the worship could begin!

But wherever there are those, however few, who gather themselves together in the Name and Presence of Jesus and accept the greatest of all equations, 'Jesus = Lord', there you have the Church. His Spirit fills the Church. In Dr Newton

Flew's delightful dictum, 'The Church is the home of the Holy Spirit'. All our love of Church order and discipline must not make us lose sight of the simplicity of Christ's way with men. He is able to found His Church where and when He pleases. A German pastor once told me that he was travelling in China and wished to pass into a territory for which he had no visa. He had not enough knowledge of the Chinese language to explain to the little official at the frontier what was the nature of his work as a Christian minister, but in the course of his stumbling explanations, he used the name of Jesus. The face of the little Chinaman crumpled into a smile. He patted the pastor, then patted himself, saying 'You, Jesus; me, Jesus!' and the Church was there then.

There is every evidence that our Lord made provision to deal with any *loneliness* in His followers.

> *Two are better far than one*
> *For counsel or for fight;*
> *How can one be warm alone,*
> *Or serve his God aright?*
> *Join we then our hearts and hands,*
> *Each to love provoke his friend;*
> *Run the way of his commands,*
> *And keep it to the end.*
>
> *Woe to him whose spirits droop,*
> *To him who falls alone!*
> *He has none to lift him up*
> *To help his weakness on:*
> *Who of twain hath made us one*
> *Maintains our unity,*
> *Jesus is our cornerstone*
> *In whom we all agree.*

The teaching of St Paul in this matter is that we are members joined to the Head. It was not merely that people came together to discuss Jesus. But as members of Christ's Church, they had heard Him and obeyed Him when He said: 'Come unto me and I will make you.' This is why no one but Christ can be considered Head of the Church. Ask James, the Lord's brother at Jerusalem: 'Who is Head of the Church at Jerusalem?' Ask Peter at Rome, Paul at Corinth, and with one voice they will say: We have one Lord as surely as we have one Faith and one Baptism. While Churchmen shuffle for places and positions in Christ's Church they are forgetting that all that matters is that we are each 'with Him'.

(3) 'BE YE SEPARATE . . .'

The Church is the congregation of the Elect. There were certain military units during the last war which were called into being for special purposes—the Commandos, the Pathfinders, the Fleet Air Arm, the R.A.F. Regiment. I saw something of some of these under training. One aspect of their preparation for active service was that it was drilled into them (literally!) that they were a special force close-knit in loyalty and manœuvrability, and an *esprit de corps* was encouraged to an exceptional degree, the reason being that for effectiveness they had to be trained to be specialists.

Israel as we have seen in Chapter 6 had been called out as a separate clan for a special purpose. Ordinances were laid down to keep her pure for God's service.

To no less a degree Jesus called men and challenged them to make themselves totally manœuvrable to His will. It is noticeable how often He called them apart to drill them in His service. Many were called but few responded to His call since His demands were so high. The modern Church is still finding it no easy thing to recruit. It may be that part of our trouble is that we are not sufficiently exacting in our demands. We glory in broadmindedness until we do the mental splits! We cling to Christ's 'he that is not against me', and forget His 'he that is not for me'. People are either in or outside the Church. They cannot be half-in and half-out as so many try to be. If we think of just three of the metaphors for the Church in the New Testament—Body, Bride, Building ('a holy temple') (1 Cor 12²⁷, Jn 3²⁹, Eph 2²¹)—we see immediately that each of these is a definite entity. We do not read that the Church is a cloud!

It is no easy question this. We find Jesus in John 17 praying for those 'whom Thou hast given me out of the world' and praying also that they be 'not taken out of the world'. But He goes on to pray that they may be kept from the evil.

Paul appears to deal with this problem in a two-fold way; first, by urging each individual member consistently to ask himself whether his manner of life tends to 'edify' the Church. Does it build up the Building? (1 Cor 14²⁶, 2 Cor 12¹⁹, Eph 4²⁹). Paul is careful not to load too many restrictions upon his fellow converts. In the main a Christian must have a sense of personal responsibility for keeping himself uncontaminated from the world. The second way Paul deals with this problem is to stress by example and precept that it is the *mutual* responsibility of the fellowship to keep one another true to the Church's calling, 'to know her election'. She is as St Peter says 'an elect race', 'a royal priesthood', and as such must keep herself unspotted from the world. (Some of us have known the discipline of a Methodist Class Meeting where fellow members have been ready to cauterize our errors!)

Dr Horton in an admirable short study of the early Church, now long out of print, says of the Church's internal discipline: 'The passage 1 Corinthians 5, is the *locus classicus*. The community was to keep itself pure. A member who was a fornicator, covetous, an idolater, a reviler, a drunkard, or an extortioner, was to be cut off from the community. The essential idea of the church was a holy brotherhood; the Communion or common meal was the expression of a new society living, as compared with that old pagan world, on higher ground, guided by nobler principles. We have nothing to do in these early days with the infliction of temporal punishments, or with that appalling engine of medieval despotism, the handing over of the delinquent to the secular arm; but the society, based on the person and teaching of Christ, is bound to eject from its borders those who refuse obedience to Him.'

Paul himself is ready to endure all things for the elect's sake

F

(2 Tim 2¹⁰). He begs his readers at Colossae: 'Put on therefore, as God's elect, holy and beloved, a heart of compassion'
(Col 3¹²).

(4) 'TAKE, EAT . . .'

The Church is the family of God sustained at His Table. When
we consider the tragedy of the fact that the divided Church
meets Christ at separate tables, we may well marvel at His
grace that He does not withhold His Body and Blood until we
are ready to sit together. We ourselves as hosts would not
feel very patient towards guests who came to supper and said:
'I am sorry, but my wife and I cannot eat with the Browns.
We will have ours over by the window.' This is tragically, if
satirically, true to the facts as they are. Every Sunday the
grace of our Lord Jesus Christ is tested and proved again when
He patiently indulges us in whims that we allow to loom larger
than love.

Yet the Church has no life but the life of Christ. He has
appointed a means of grace at His table; it is not an altar, but
it is a trysting place for us, and if we are to have the mind of
Christ we need to keep near to the heart of the Gospel and to
draw near to the place where He vouchsafes to feed us with
the spiritual food of His most precious Body and Blood.

The sanctity of this fellowship meal was marred on that
first night in which He took bread. One had a devil and went
out into the darkness. It was a terrible foreshadowing of the
shallowness of Christian fellowship that the disciples in turn
round the table had to ask 'Is it I?', though in charity one must
admit that it was also a sign of the humility we all need to feel
when we partake. Each one of us has a devil and cannot pre-
sume to come trusting in his own righteousness, but in His
great and manifold mercy.

Paul has terrible things to say to those who do not take the
Lord's Supper sufficiently seriously. By their bad manners—
not even worthy of a dinner party at home—they are eating to
their own damnation; they are 'guilty of the body and blood
of the Lord' (1 Cor 11²⁷).

Paul writes on the assumption that the practice of partaking of the Lord's Supper is already universal. This is of the utmost importance to our belief that Christ really did intend this meal to be a permanent factor of the Church's life. It is amazing and shocking that in Nonconformity we sometimes give the impression that attendance at Holy Communion is an optional extra.

It is certain that Paul looked on Christ's table as a bond of the fellowship. In a mystery beyond our grasping, even as we *take* His Body we *are* His Body. This brings with it the responsibility of caring for those at the same table with us. What does our Lord think of Church members who go on for years not even considering it a matter of courtesy that they should get to know those who are bound to them in this most sacred sacramentum? Or do we think it right to follow the publicans (*sic*), who do not expect those who drink at the same counter to have fellowship with one another unless it suits them.

(5) 'HE APPOINTED SOME . . .'

The Church is one working band, one army strong. There are two good rules for a Christian—put Christ in His place (and as John R. Mott said, 'Make sure it is the first place') and then find the place where He puts *you.* Christ has many services to be done. That was why He chose a varied group of first apostles; that was why He chose Peter and Paul, who were so different. After a certain amount of tension, they came to recognize that Christ had a special function for each of them to fulfil.

It is stimulating to watch how many different services Jesus called forth. The use of a boat, a lodging, a donkey, the provision of a drink of water at the well, an upper room, a seamless robe, the loan—and it was only a loan—of five loaves and two fishes, and in the end the use of two beams of wood. So in the work of redeeming the world, He calls upon the many members of His Body, each in their several capacities. So far as I can gather, there are about thirteen 'offices' mentioned in Paul's epistles: apostle, prophet, evangelist, pastor, teacher, deacon, exhorter, giver, administrator, healer, miracle-worker, helper, speaker in tongues. (If he had added a few more, many would still include them all in the duties of a Methodist minister!) Ought we not to take more pains, individually and collectively, to discover what gifts Christ has given to what people, and see that they are suitably placed? It would give a shock if some Church decided that a certain man might be a better caterer at tea meetings than 'the Ladies'! My own conviction is that in all our Churches we have hidden gifts of the Spirit, charismatic blessings intended for us all, which we are failing to call forth. Are we really listening to the voice of the Spirit just now, as He reminds us that some have been given the gift of healing? We need shaking out of our conventional grooves of thought. What matters is that Christ calls each man to serve as each man can. 'What about *him* Lord?' 'What is that to thee? Follow *thou* me!' It is the same lesson that Paul is teaching when he paints the ludicrous picture of the hand and the ear and the nose quarrelling about their individual functions.

(6) 'GO YE INTO ALL THE WORLD!'

The Church exists for those outside her borders. It is not long in the ministry of Jesus before we find Him saying: 'Let us go elsewhere into the next towns, that I may preach there also; for to this end came I forth' (Mk 1³⁸). To press on to the next opportunity to 'administer bliss' is a hall-mark of those who have the mind of Christ. Dr Johnson was irritated by John Wesley's inability to sit leisurely and drink a dish of tea, but he was in the presence of one who was a true evangelist in the steps of his Master. 'To this end have I been born, and to this end am I come into the world, that I should bear witness unto the truth' (Jn 18³⁷). And so long as there is any ignorance needing the truth, any darkness waiting for light, the Spirit of Christ will be driving His own. One sometimes feels tempted to pronounce a revised benediction on a congregation—'May the restlessness of God abide in your hearts.'

When Jesus commissioned His first apostles, He was in

effect commissioning all who should believe through them. In reference to the Resurrection appearance where Jesus said 'Peace be unto you; as the Father hath sent me, even so send I you. . . . Receive ye the Holy Ghost' (Jn 20²¹⁻²²), Bishop Westcott cryptically remarks: 'The commission must be regarded properly as the commission of the Christian Society and not as that of the Christian Ministry.' As we shall see later, the whole society of the Church is part of Christ's ministry, and it is a ministry to the whole world. If we join the Church, we join a Missionary Society.

Paul the Missionary—What a standard he sets us! What energy, what tenacity, what determination to go on and on to preach good tidings to the poor, to proclaim release to the captives, the recovery of sight to the blind, to set at liberty them that are bruised, to proclaim the acceptable year of the Lord! He can't stop, even though he is in half a mind to want to depart and be for ever with the Lord.

There must have been some very special reason to keep him tethered at Ephesus (Acts 19¹⁰) 'for the space of two years'. There were some there who were 'hardened and disobedient speaking evil of the Way before the multitude'. It may well be that his concentrated work there brought the fruit that is represented in the circular letter written to the Ephesians, but in general practice Paul's motto was 'I press on'.

I was speaking a short while ago to a missionary. He told me that on his return to England his most serious impression of the Church here in these days has been of its lack of *urgency*. Though our heart is at peace we ought not to rest until we die. Catherine Booth said as she was dying '. . . and I did so want to do more for the prisoners'. Let us enjoy Christian fellowship; let us perfect the saints; but never for a moment let us forget that there are those who do not yet the Saviour know. We may feel we have reached the height of bliss by having ourselves been saved, but there is still some sinner over whose repentance Heaven waits to rejoice. As the gasping casualty said to the warden, who dragged him from the rubble: 'There's another chap inside.'

CHAPTER EIGHT

My Ministry

God gave unto us the ministry of reconciliation (2 Cor 5¹⁸)

THERE IS something childish, and not admirably so, if we are obsessed with the particular part which we ourselves are playing in the drama of the Kingdom. A child in an insignificant part in the school entertainment can see little importance in anyone else's share in the whole production. What matters is *my* part, *my* lines, *my* entrance, *my* exit, *my* costume, and above all, *my* applause from the audience. This may be understandable and excusable in a child; in an adult it is pitiable. But what Christian is wholly free from this brand of egotism? *Our* corner of the vineyard, or whatever trite phrase we may care to use, is all-important. If we could but see our greatest endeavours in the setting of the whole picture, we should discover that it is as nothing more than a quarter-inch fleck from one pig's bristle of one paint brush on the huge canvas of a Rembrandt painting. So when we talk about *our* ministry, *our* term of office, *our* career, as though these were of great significance, God must smile. If people would read a little more history they would have a better sense of proportion in viewing the little saga of their own contribution.

Yet it is clear that St Paul has an awareness of his own ministry as an entity in itself. From the vantage point of a later century, we can see how that ministry was of supreme importance in the history of mankind. It was to affect the whole trend of events. That concentrated offering of twenty or thirty years of dramatic life was to be more than a little speck on the canvas. But it is not in boastful terms that Paul is thinking when he speaks of 'my work in the Lord' (1 Cor 9¹), 'my service' (Rom 15³¹), 'the ministry which I have received' (Acts 20²⁴). He has no false modesty, and he goes into the attack for the next battle with as much zest as an advancing general would announce to his men: 'Now, we must capture this next position, and the whole war depends on this battle.' One can imagine Paul rallying Silas on the road with something of the swagger of an actor on the stage: 'We meet at Philippi.' But what St Paul would *not* say is that it was *his* war or *his* victory. The egoists in wartime who talked about *their* bomb, and *their* injury, usually went on to talk about *their* war! But for St Paul it was the Ministry of Christ which was paramount and into that Ministry he had been called.

This brings us to the Protestant doctrine of the Ministry. It has perhaps been nowhere better or more simply expressed than by Dr T. W. Manson in *The Church's Ministry:* 'There is only one "essential ministry" in the Church, the perpetual ministry of the Risen and Ever-Present Lord Himself. All other ministries are derivative, dependent and functional. All ministries are functions exercised by the Body of Christ through organs which are organs of the Body. Consequently, it is the Church which is apostolic, and the apostle is an organ of the Church.' In other words, we are given a place in the Ministry of Christ, and by His grace we may share in it.

In this sense—and it is the only true New Testament interpretation—all those who are 'in Christ' are in His ministry. There is an interesting sidelight on this to be seen at the beginning of Ephesians 4[12], in the description of the gifts of the ascended Christ, in the various functions to be fulfilled. We have been accustomed to read: 'for the perfecting of the saints, unto the work of ministering', with a dividing comma. Later editions—starting, I believe, with the B.F.B.S. edition of Nestle's Greek Testament—have made it clear that what Paul said was this: 'for the perfecting of the saints for the work of the ministry'—all the saints are in the ministry!

Now let it be said straight away that this is not to sell the pass in the matter of an ordained Ministry for special functions of Word and Sacrament. The Church believes that the Holy Spirit is given to those whom she believes God has specially called and to whom He has given special gifts for prophecy, evangelism, pastoral work, teaching, governments, etc. What we need to realize is that calling and endowments are needed for many other tasks and many varied spheres. We are not wrong to dedicate Sunday School teachers, and Youth workers, and servants of the Missionary Cause. We might do well to go farther and realize that the blessing of the Church and the perfecting of the saints is desperately needed for the work of the ministry of Christ in factories and business offices. It need not only be in an ironical or metaphorical sense that the modern Christian sings: 'Ye servants of the Lord, each in his office wait!'

A certain distinguished worker in the Church Overseas began his missionary service as a young teacher in West Africa. When he left his home Church in a conventional London suburb, he was asked by the leaders of that Church if he would like to have a Service of Dedication before he left. He replied that he would, but only on condition that his friend, Leonard, was also given the same honour and glory and blessing. Now Leonard was going into a local engineering factory on the Great West Road. This was too much of a stretch of vision for the leaders concerned, and the matter was left in abeyance. This probably meant that those leaders had an inadequate conception of the ministry of Christ.

We are quite sure that to be a Christian teacher in a Missionary Station is a dedicated task. Many still need to be convinced that to be a carpenter is the sort of work Jesus Christ still wants done in His Spirit and to His glory. It would almost seem that we have limited the word 'calling' to the three-fold public ministries of Jesus as teacher, preacher, and 'leecher'. To teach, preach, heal—this is the work of Christ; but to dig, weave, sow and reap—these are merely 'jobs'; and whilst needing chaplains to establish contact with those who perform them, we are still feeling our way to understanding how such tasks can be a full Christian vocation. We seem to be able to grasp (on Sunday night) the idea of giving a cup of cold water in Christ's name, but after a night's sleep we are a little vague about the man in the Corporation water-works who sees that the water is fit to drink, and the man in the Town Council sewage works who disposes of what we do not want. To be completely honest, Paul on Mars Hill was probably doing a more important work than when he was sewing the seams of a tent, but did he not himself say: '*Whatsoever* you do, work heartily, as unto the Lord, and not unto men' (Col 3²³).

Let us now examine the essential elements in Christ's conception of His ministry and St Paul's out-working of these ideas.

(1) JESUS KNEW HIMSELF TO BE CHOSEN AND CALLED—SO DID ST PAUL

No one has dared to say what Jesus said: 'Before Abraham was, I am.' The choice of Jesus as our Saviour was before the foundation of the world. There was a point in time when it was hardest of all to understand how He could be 'the Son whom God hath appointed heir of all things' (Heb 1²). No wonder that His enemies cried at the foot of the Cross: 'Let him save himself if he is the Christ whom God has chosen.' But it was this awareness of being the Chosen of His Father which sustained Jesus against all the powers of evil. At His baptism He knew that there was no escape from that choice, and it was a voice from Heaven, even more than the sorrows of mankind calling forth His compassion, which constituted His call.

It was not an uncommon experience for the prophets to have the conviction that they had been chosen before birth. 'The Lord hath called me from the womb', cried Isaiah. 'And the word of the Lord came to Jeremiah saying, "Before I formed thee in the belly, I knew thee, and before thou camest forth out of the womb, I sanctified thee".'

St Paul is in this category of men. He says to the Galatians: 'God separated me even from my mother's womb, and called me through his grace, to reveal his Son in me' (Gal 1¹⁵). He did not *decide* to be a Christian preacher; he was 'called to be an apostle'. A young man once said to an older: 'I want to be a local preacher', and had the reply: 'That's very good, young man, but are you *called?* Are you *called?*' Paul was a 'born preacher' if ever there was one. Would that all the Lord's people were born preachers! For St Paul would not have us believe that it was a monopoly of his own to be elect; the weak and the foolish, as well as the noble and mighty, are chosen to put to shame the things that are strong. To be in the ministry of Christ in any sphere or capacity whatsoever involves the reverent acceptance of this ministry, that we are chosen of God, a chosen generation, an elect race.

(2) JESUS KNEW THAT HE HAD BEEN SENT— SO DID ST PAUL

The ministry of Jesus was one sustained fulfilment of a commission the Father had given Him. The things that He did were done because He had been *sent* to do them. He had been *sent* to Israel and *sent* for the salvation of the world. So to His apostles He said: 'As the Father hath sent me, so send I you.'

As St Paul entered a strange town, what were his credentials? He claimed no 'authority' such as he had when he went up and down the land persecuting the Christians with a warrant for their arrest. He had no diploma from the college of Rabbis, for his doctrines were heresy in every Jewish synagogue that he entered. Rome did not own him, though they acknowledged that he had certain rights as a free citizen. But in his heart he carried a writ; and that was the inner witness that he had been *sent*. It is this secret document written in Christ's own handwriting which keeps all His servants confident in any circumstances, and free from the fear of what men may do to them. To be in the ordained Ministry of the Church without having this inner commission must be a soul-destroying life. But if you have it, the certainty that you are sent with a message and have a purpose enables you to press on, to lay hold of that for which Christ laid hold on you.

To think again of Paul entering a strange town—one wonders whether His desire for independence in the matter of receiving payment arose not so much out of pride as from a basic desire to make it plain that he came in Christ's employ and not a paid teacher. He was sent with a Gospel to give away, not with a panacea to sell. When he preached the Gospel 'he made the gospel without charge' (1 Cor 9^{18}). This was no insignificant matter to Paul, and he followed his Master's mind scrupulously. Had not Jesus said, 'Freely ye received, freely give.' So Paul worked at tent-making in order that his own hands should minister to his own necessities (Acts 18^3, 20^{34}). He coveted no man's silver or gold. He worked night and day among the people of Thessalonica, in order that he might not be a burden to any of them while he was preaching the Gospel of God (1 Thess 2^9).

But had not the Master also said that the labourer was worthy of his hire, in the sense that even an ox treading the corn is given food (Lk 10^7, Deut 25^4)? There is every sign that Jesus was entertained and enjoyed that hospitality with the apparent relish of a gluttonous man and a wine-bibber (Lk 7^{34}). He accepted the services of those who ministered to Him and gave Him hospitality in their homes. Even so, says Paul, did the Lord ordain that they which proclaim the gospel should live of the gospel (1 Cor 9^{14}). There is no sophistry here, no fiddling of the expense account. He was not paid, but with his Master he was not too proud to be given hospitality. 'If we showed unto you spiritual things, is it a great matter if we shall reap your carnal things?' (Laymen please note that a Methodist minister receives an allowance or stipend, but not a wage or salary.)

If Paul had been made an apostle by the choice of God rather than by the will of men, he knew that it was also God's choice *where* he should be sent. Peter had been premature in his avowal that he was ready to go both to prison and to death for Jesus. But St Paul meant this promise and kept it, and in the process he did not lose his certainty of being commissioned wherever he was sent. He is nowhere more like his Master than in his own joyful acceptance of the *locale* of his ministry— *sent* to jail, *sent* into the storm, *sent* to the whipping post, *sent* into the wilderness, 'sent to Coventry', but sent. In that sending his mind was at peace. An old man who was in a mental home, but who was sane enough to believe in Jesus and testify to Him, said to me: 'I think I am *needed* here.' What a vision, and what Christian discipline! My own mother, dying in discomfort in an accident ward, lying on a miserable mattress with at least five people in trouble on her hands around her, said in the last conversation I had with her: 'You know, Derrick, I think there is something I can do here.'

(3) JESUS WAS CHOSEN AND SENT TO BE A SERVANT— AND SO WAS PAUL

Among the many startling sayings of Jesus we shall always include His statement that He came not to be ministered unto, but to minister. This was a strange claim from one who was ready to be called Master. It was, of course, a total rejection of the world's wisdom whereby progress to success involves an increasing capacity to have things done for you. The modern man of the Western world would be shocked if it was suggested that he was little different from the tribal chieftain who estimates his wealth in slaves. Yet what is money but the wherewithal to buy goods and *services?* The coldest fact about Western economics at the moment is that a Prime Minister (or the Queen's First Servant) can assert that we have 'never had it so good', and go on to interpret 'the good' in terms of the things that money can buy. The successful man in the eyes of the world has enough goods to be able to take his ease and be waited upon. But Jesus has shown us that the best people, the top people, are those who are on the serving side of the counter.

The ministry of Jesus involved the full commitments of a slave of the time. When He took a towel and girded Himself, it was only a symbolic act of a much deeper commitment as a servant of His Father, and as a servant of men for His Father's sake. To be a slave meant that you were body and soul possessed by your owner, you were completely at his disposal day and night. You might have privileges and kudos as the slave of a certain notable man, but you were liable to be asked to do anything that he wanted done; you might have to wait on him at table, and even risk your life by first tasting his wine; you were his hands and feet, and you were liable to be asked to carry him to save his legs. You also had to serve anyone he wanted served, whether you liked them or not. You were his watchdog, his pillow, his alarm clock, his tools; you were his runner and his messenger; and when danger came, you were his shield and defence, for, if occasion arose, your life must be taken rather than his. After saying all this, it is worth noting that many slaves were happy. If they had a fine master it was their greatest boast to be called 'the general's personal servant'.

So St Paul was proud to be a servant of Jesus Christ. The Master Himself had been all that Isaiah had described as the 'Suffering Servant'. To be in the ministry of Christ was to serve a Lord who had entered fully into every aspect of service, and the least of the apostles was ready to vie with anyone for first place as personal slave to Jesus Christ. The Pope is proud to be called 'The Servant of the Servants of God'.

There was one aspect of this life of a servant which is specially to be noted. Paul looked on himself, as the servant of men for Jesus's sake. How can we serve Christ at the point where we are serving other people? This is a question that many pose when they long to have a sense of Christian vocation in the ordinary duties of life. Is it a merely fanciful pseudo-mystical idea that we can sweep a room for God, or that inasmuch as we do something for one of His brethren, we are doing it for Him? Far from being fanciful, I believe it is the most practical thing that Jesus ever said and far more simple than we make it.

Look at it in two elementary ways. It is possible for a shop assistant to serve a customer and at the same time to be in the service of his employer (whom he may never have met). In serving the customer he *is* serving his employer. So it is possible for a Christian to serve his fellows and at the same time to be serving Christ.

Their earthly task who fail to do,
Neglect their heavenly business too,
Nor know what faith and duty mean,
Who use religion as a screen,
Asunder put what God hath joined,
A diligent and pious mind.

Full well the labour of our hands
With fervency of spirit stands;
For God, who all our days hath given,
From toil excepts but one in seven:
And labouring while we time redeem,
We please the Lord, and work for Him.

Or again, if you think of someone you love very much, the fact of your loving them involves your weeping when they weep, and rejoicing when they rejoice. If you *hate* them, you will weep when they rejoice, and rejoice when they weep. That is one of the many differences between love and hate. Such is love that when a child is hurt the mother says that the pain 'goes through her'. Someone once asked Charlotte Brontë: 'How are you?' and she replied: 'I have a pain in my sister's right side.' As Christ loves all the world, it is understandable that He is hurt when anyone in the world is hurt, and when parched lips are moistened, He is less thirsty.

To be in the ministry of Christ for Paul or for any of us means that we share Christ's honoured title of Servant of Men. We count as religious acts not only those times when we share in what we call Divine Service, but also all the common or garden occasions when we do something which our Master wants done.

(4) JESUS WAS CHOSEN AND SENT AS A SERVANT IN THE MINISTRY OF RECONCILIATION— AND SO WAS PAUL

In the hymns of Charles Wesley we find reference to the work of Christ as the Ambassador sent from the Father:

His kind invitation, ye sinners embrace,
Accepting salvation, salvation by grace.
Sent down from above, who governs the skies
In vehement love to sinners He cries.

We hear this Gospel of salvation through ambassadors who
beseech us on behalf of Christ 'Be ye reconciled to God'.

God, the offended God most high,
Ambassadors to rebels sends;
His messengers his place supply,
And Jesus begs us to be friends.

Us, in the stead of Christ, they pray,
Us, in the stead of God, intreat,
To cast our arms, our sins, away,
And find forgiveness at his feet.

So each ambassador in his turn, has within himself the
assurance that he is God's personal messenger.

My message as from God receive,
Ye all may come to Christ, and live;
O let his love your hearts constrain
Nor suffer him to die in vain!

What does the Cross signify? Well, it is the cross-beams
of wood on which Jesus was *stretched*. That is a terrible truth,
since He died as a result of the breath being pressed from
His lungs, as His body was torn apart. The crossbeams speak
of His outstretched arms of love, holding together the opposing forces of the world. There is poignant irony in the fact
that at the very time of His dying, the Pharisees and the mob
had made an unholy pact together, and that 'Herod and Pilate
became friends with each other that very day: for before
they were at enmity between themselves' (Lk 23¹²). Christ's
pact to reconcile men to one another knows no limit. This is
our only hope in a world on the brink of war. He and He only
can bring together the opposing forces of mankind. His arms
are outstretched far enough to circle the earth.

But it is the upright beam which has the greater significance for His work of reconciliation. This stretched from Heaven to earth, from earth to Heaven. As our Mediator, Christ came down to earth, came to reach the lowest and the least; in fact it is our creedal confession that His love reaches so far down that it can touch even the souls in Hell. But this same Tree of Life reaches up to Heaven for us. It is the Jacob's Ladder of all men's dreams; and we shall come to Heaven only as we cling to Him who descends and ascends for our soul's salvation.

We may well pause here so that we may worship Christ whose ministry to us has been to give us complete access to God. His outstretched arms, His downstretched body, is the only proof we need of the fact that there is nothing to separate us from the love of God.

Now Paul dares to suggest that Christ has called him even into *this* ministry. 'All things are of God, who reconciled us to himself through Christ, and gave unto us the ministry of reconciliation' (2 Cor 5[18]). Paul was only too aware that it involved the stretching of all his powers. Just at the human level, it involved that work of peace-maker between quarrelsome individuals. St Paul yearned over a young church that was being torn apart by divisions and disputes. To mention only two: he did his best to reconcile Syntyche and Euodia, and Philemon and Onesimus. He was a wonderful pastor because he knew he must share Christ's work as a reconciler. A broken fellowship is always a challenge to any minister of Christ; and a heart-breaking, back-breaking business it is.

But Paul also shared in that eternal tug between the love of God and the sin of men. As a man of God he cried: 'We are ambassadors on behalf of Christ, as though God were intreating by us: we beseech you on behalf of Christ, be ye reconciled to God' (2 Cor 5[20]); and at the same time as a man alongside his fellow sinners, he never ceased to give thanks to God for the riches of His mercy, in having opened up a way of reconciliation through Christ.

Here is to be seen the true pattern for the whole ministry of

the Church and every member in it. Our worship involves
God's coming down to us and our reaching up to God. Those
in the ordained Ministry know something of what this means.
A minister of Christ must be a man of God and a man of the
world. He must be a good mystic and a good mixer. He must
be holy and hearty. He must be 'insulated', in the sense that
his power and effectiveness depend upon his keeping unin-
terrupted contact with spiritual resources. Yet he must be
'earthed', in the sense that his feet are on the ground and his
sermons down to earth. He must be equally at home on the
mount and with the multitude.

But is this not true of *all* who are in Christ? Is this not true
of *all* who have the mind of Christ? They are committed with
Him to a ministry that ranges between earth and Heaven.
That is why one takes off one's clerical hat to the simple (and
yet wise) Christians in the humdrum round of bread-winning
who so maintain the spiritual glow that they are in fact living
representatives of the Christ who is Mediator between earth
and Heaven.

G

CHAPTER NINE

My Sufferings

I rejoice in my sufferings (Col 1^{24})

DR RUSSELL MALTBY once poked fun at the man who has to live with his mother-in-law and insists on talking about 'his cross'. St Paul, who had more than his fair share of cross-bearing, dismissed all his sufferings 'on the behalf of Christ', much as an old soldier might speak of the exigencies of the Service. He took his share of hardness gladly and merely talked about his 'light affliction which was for the moment'.

The tone of voice in which he seems to have spoken of his physical and spiritual tests of endurance was much more like the tone of one who speaks quite calmly of his duty, or his difficult appointment, or his share of responsibility in any particular undertaking. These things were all very much to be expected. Even his thorn in the flesh is not spoken about in the way some people refer to 'my neuritis', or 'my head', or 'my problem'. It was simply a weakness in which he found glory (2 Cor 12$^{7-10}$).

Yet Paul is only too well aware that as a soldier of Jesus Christ he is going to suffer under the same slings and arrows as the Captain of his salvation. He speaks of his suffering as an integral factor of Christian service. My afflictions, my persecutions, my tribulations, my temptations, my wants, my necessities, my bonds, my chains, my infirmities—they are all mine; but since I am Christ's, these also are Christ's sufferings which happen to spill over into my body. Life and death and all things are mine, and I am Christ's. It is this that makes all suffering for Christ's sake not only bearable, but honourable and even glorious. Even a thorn in the flesh can be used as an instrument of His grace.

This pain, this consecrated pain,
    With which my soul and flesh are filled,
His instrument if He ordain,
    The pure and perfect love shall yield;
But by whatever means 'tis done,
    The work and praise are all His own.

To be joined to Christ is to take risks, and no true follower of His asks: 'What are the minimum conditions of membership?' Jesus Christ is as frank with his followers as any military leader. No Garibaldi or Winston Churchill ever spoke more explicitly about conditions of enlistment. To be identified with Jesus means no mere acceptance of a political programme or school of philosophy. 'Christ in me' means that Christ crucified is in me. Every time He beckons or points or reaches out to help me, it is with hands marked by the wound prints; there is no Christianity without tears.

I once went to ask Warburton Lewis for his advice about books. He suddenly said to me: 'What is the most exciting text in the Bible?' My mind ranged over such phrases as: 'Suddenly there was with the angels . . .' or 'Suddenly there came from Heaven a sound . . .' or 'Suddenly there shone round about him . . . a light'. He stopped me and said—'I have been crucified with Christ'. As a placard for a Sunday morning paper this would stand alone and make 'I was Eichmann's batman' look like something from *Home Chat!*

But when you come to think of it, this was the only way that Paul could describe his experience. His life was, with St Peter's, the first great experiment in trusting Jesus all the way. If they had persecuted Jesus, they were going to persecute Paul, and that was that. The terms of enrolment had promised no less. Jesus had warned His disciples that what happened to Him would, in some way or other, happen to them. This had been Christ's promise, not merely His warning. For to suffer with Him means that we shall also be glorified with Him. 'The afflictions which ye endure,' he says, are 'a manifest token of the righteous judgement of God; to the end that ye may be counted worthy of the Kingdom of God, for which ye also suffer (2 Thess 1⁴⁻⁵). If men hated Christ's face and saw to it that His image was marred, they are not going to like the look of us if we remind them of Him. If no suffering for Christ's sake is coming our way, it is time that we asked ourselves how far we have lost His likeness. It was a shrewd judgement of the Anglican Report in 1948 on the Conversion of England, which said: 'It is hard to know whether the Church is not to be condemned more for its failure to repel than for its failure to attract.'

To have the mind of Christ involves sharing His *compassion*. This is only another way of saying that we *suffer with* anyone who suffers. Some Christians strike the world as serious and humourless. This is not always because their light is burning rather dimly, but sometimes rather because they feel acutely over matters which do not cause any concern to those who do not know Christ. Christians constantly recognize as 'social problems' evils which others accept as normal. The Christian conscience is stirred to pity or wrath, and in order that the evil may be eradicated, there is the inevitable process of costly redemption. (To suffer with Christ in the modern world often means that you have to suffer innumerable committees and interminable cyclostyled memoranda.) Hong Kong refugees are not saved by human pity alone; they are saved by pity which issues in the long-drawn-out process of getting things done and putting things right. And in such matters the non-Christian often puts the Christian to shame.

Again, to have the Mind of Christ involves bearing Christ's *shame*. Christ Himself had despised the shame involved in taking upon Himself the likeness of men. Common loyalty demands that when we have accepted His work for our acquittal we shall be ready to identify ourselves with Him at the point where men gainsay Him. To do otherwise is to be like a man who makes use of his minister as a defending witness in the magistrate's court, but who then refuses to own his association with a dog-collar when the minister visits the factory where he works! To do so would be to receive a share

of the jibes against the minister. A large part of Paul's suffering was straightforward honest-to-goodness loyalty in standing
by the Lord, who had stood by him. This involved calumny
and violence, and jibes that were like barbed arrows, but the
fiery darts of the Evil One were aimed at Christ far more
than at Paul, and it was part of the glory of being in Christ's
retinue that his own robe got spattered with blood.

> *And shall I slight my Father's love?*
>   *Or basely fear His gifts to own?*
> *Unmindful of His favours prove?*
>   *Shall I, the hallowed cross to shun,*
> *Refuse his righteousness to impart,*
>   *By hiding it within my heart?*
>
> *No! though the ancient dragon rage,*
>   *And call forth all his host to war,*
> *Though earth's self-righteous sons engage,*
>   *Them and their god alike I dare;*
> *Jesus, the sinner's Friend, proclaim;*
>   *Jesus, to sinners still the same.*

Few of us in twentieth-century Britain have known these
depths and heights of loyalty to Christ. It has been our
questionable fortune to have lived in a generation which has
tolerated or ignored us, and if it has at times hated us, the
hatred has been in a restrained way, barely vocal, let alone
violent. It is true that to suffer shame for Christ's sake still
means that many a typist is ready to be taunted because she
is a Sunday School teacher, and one does not underestimate
the discomfort of being in Christ's stead in barrack room,
council chamber, sports pavilion, fish shop, common room,
and so on. But we are both ignorant and innocent if we
imagine that contemporary persecution for Christ's sake bears
much resemblance to that suffered by our fathers. For one
thing, men have died for the Faith so that *we* should not have
to die for the Faith.

I want now to do a rather dangerous thing. The sufferings of

St Paul bear a quite extraordinary likeness to those of his Saviour. I want to recount them alongside one another. They do not occur necessarily in identical order, but the nature of them is strikingly similar. All this must not be taken to imply that a man cannot be a Christian unless he undergoes scourging and death. There is a sense in which real suffering is the same in whatever guise it is endured. I once knew a man who was suffering from a painful disease. He told me that when people visited him it did not worry him at all if they had not endured his particular complaint, but he said he always knew within five minutes if they had suffered in some form. The important fact to remember is that you cannot truly have the Mind of Christ and identify yourself with Him unless you are prepared to suffer *in some form*.

As I have said, it is a fact that for St Paul this suffering took on a startling affinity to that of Christ. Here is an outline. (It is surprising, incidentally, that the Revisers in the margin to the Acts of the Apostles have included so very few references back to the ministry and passion of Jesus.)

Christ sent Paul, not to baptize, but to preach the Gospel (1 Cor 1[17]). The times of ignorance God had overlooked, but now He was commanding all men everywhere to repent (Acts 17[30]). It was Paul's custom to arrive in a city 'teaching and preaching the word of the Lord (Acts 15[35]).

'Jesus began to preach, and to say, Repent ye' (Mt 4[17]).

'Jesus went about through cities and villages, preaching and bringing the good tidings of the kingdom of God' (Lk 8[1]).

'Some mocked; but others said, We will hear thee concerning this yet again' (Acts 17[32]).

'Paul went out from among them, but certain men clave unto him, and believed' (Acts 17[33-4]).

'Some . . . said, This is of a truth the prophet. Others said, This is the Christ. But some said, What, doth the Christ come out of Galilee?' (Jn 7[40-1]).

Very early in Paul's ministry 'the Jews took counsel together to kill him'. He preached 'boldly in the name of the Lord, . . . but they went about to kill him' (Acts 9[23] and [29]).

It was his boast when he stood trial that he had kept nothing back. He had not shrunk 'from declaring . . . anything that was profitable', but had taught 'publicly, and from house to house' (Acts 20²⁰).

'I have spoken openly to the world; I ever taught in synagogues, and in the temple, where all the Jews come together; and in secret spake I nothing' (Jn 18²⁰).

'Certain men came down from Judaea' (Acts 15¹).

There were gathered together unto Jesus 'the Pharisees, and certain of the scribes, which had come from Jerusalem' (Mk 7¹).

Men said that he was 'mad' (that he had religious mania) (Acts 26²⁴).

His friends 'went out to lay hold on him: for they said, He is beside himself'. (He is in a religious ecstasy) (Mk 3²¹).

But this only made Paul the more determined to 'go bound in the spirit unto Jerusalem' (Acts 20²²).

'Jesus began to shew unto his disciples, how that he must go unto Jerusalem, and suffer many things' (Mt 16²¹).

On his way to Jerusalem, like His master, Paul continued teaching as he went (Acts 28³¹).

'He went on his way through cities and villages, teaching, and journeying on unto Jerusalem' (Lk 13²²).

He held his life to be of no account as dear unto himself, so that he might accomplish his course, the ministry which he had received from the Lord Jesus (Acts 20²⁴).

'The Son of man shall be delivered up . . . and they shall kill him' (Mt 17²²⁻³).

There are touching scenes, simple, affectionate and dignified, where Paul says goodbye to his friends among whom he had gone about preaching the Kingdom and who would see his face no more. (Compare Acts 20 and Jn 16.)

'A little while, and ye behold me no more' (Jn 16¹⁶).

Paul begged his friends from Ephesus, 'Take heed unto yourselves, and to all the flock' of God and to beware of grievous wolves. He told them, 'from among your own selves shall men arise, speaking perverse things, to draw away the disciples after them' (Acts 20²⁸⁻³⁰).

He told them that in all things he had given them an example (Acts 20³⁵).

'*Behold, I send you forth as lambs in the midst of wolves*' (Lk 10³).

'*I have given you an example*' (Jn 13¹⁵).

Paul's friends besought him not to go up to Jerusalem, but he told them that he was ready 'not to be bound only, but also to die at Jerusalem' (Acts 21¹³).

'*The Son of man must suffer many things*'. '*Peter took him and began to rebuke him*' (Mk 8³¹⁻²).

As at Athens Paul's spirit 'was provoked within him as he beheld the city full of idols' (Acts 17¹⁶), so no doubt the thought of his nation's capital city stirred him to compassion and concern.

'*And when Jesus drew nigh, He saw the city and wept over it*' (Lk 19⁴¹).

The closing chapters of the Acts reveal the same pattern of trumped-up charges and the twisting of truth such as had surrounded Paul's Master at His Passion, and his enemies could not be agreed on his guilt. In both Jesus and Paul the prophecy was fulfilled that men hated them without a case, or cause.

The assembly was divided. 'There arose a great clamour: and some of the scribes of the Pharisees' part stood up, and strove, saying, We find no evil in this man: and what if a spirit hath spoken to him, or an angel? And when there arose a great dissension, the chief captain, fearing lest Paul should be torn in pieces by them, commanded the soldiers to go down and take him by force from among them, and bring him into the castle' (Acts 23⁹⁻¹⁰).

'*The Chief Priests and the Elders of the people took counsel together that they might take Jesus by subtilty and kill Him, but they said: Not during the Feast, lest a tumult arise among the people*' (Mt 26⁴⁻⁵).

Loose charges were thrown about. Just as it had been said of Socrates that he was a perverter of the youth of Athens, so Tertullus said that 'they had found this man Paul a pestilent fellow, and a mover of insurrections among all the Jews throughout the world, and a ringleader of the sect of the Nazarenes, who moreover assayed to profane the Temple' (Acts 24⁵).

'*Many bare false witness against Jesus and their witness agreed not together. And there stood up certain and bare false witness against Him saying: We heard him say I will destroy this temple that is made with hands, and in three days I will build another made without hands. And not even so did their witness agree together*' (Mk 14⁵⁶⁻⁵⁹).

'Felix came with Drusilla his wife . . . and sent for Paul and heard him concerning the faith in Christ Jesus.' 'He hoped withal that money would be given him of Paul: wherefore he sent for him the oftener and communed with him. . . .' 'But desiring to gain favour with the Jews, Felix left Paul in bonds' (Acts 24²⁴⁻²⁷).

'*While Pilate was on the judgement-seat, his wife sent unto him*' (Mt 27¹⁹).

'*Herod hoped to see some miracle done by him*' (Lk 23⁸).

'*Pilate gave sentence that what they asked for should be done*' (Lk 23²⁴).

On one occasion 'the multitude of the people followed after, crying out, Away with him' (Acts 21³⁶).

And on another his fathers and brethren 'lifted up their voice and said: Away with such a fellow from the earth, for it is not fit that he should live' (Acts 22²²).

'They therefore cried out, Away with him, away with him, crucify him' (Jn 19¹⁵).

'*They were instant with loud voice, asking that He might be crucified*' (Lk 23²³).

But through it all, no one was able to present a clear proven charge. Paul would never have claimed to be innocent in the sense that Jesus was, that is, without spot or blemish, but he was not guilty of any crime worthy of death. He protested to the Governor Felix 'that neither in the temple did they find him disputing with any man or stirring up a crowd. Neither could they prove the things whereof they accused him.' It was touching the resurrection of the dead that he was called in question (Acts 24$^{12-21}$).

Agrippa admitted to Festus that this man might have been set at liberty if he had not appealed to Caesar. They both agreed that he had done nothing worthy of death or bonds (Acts 26$^{31-2}$).

And the issue? This was to be death. Of that death there is no account. Why was no vivid record left to us of the last sufferings of this blessed apostle who had so faithfully followed his Master's steps along his own Via Dolorosa? Surely because nothing must distract our eyes from the one and only figure on a Cross by which men should be saved. Was it not of divine purpose that no account has been left to us of Paul's martyrdom lest any man should glory save in the death of Christ. Paul least of all would have boasted of his own cross.

Paul's progress to glory has been repeated in the lives of more saints than could be numbered. But his own story is an amazing commentary on the total identification of a man with the way of Christ. He shared Christ's travail and he shared Christ's triumph. Through it all he shared that quality of Christlikeness which Baron von Hügel used to say was an indispensable factor in the life of a saint; he was 'radiant in the midst of the strain and stress of life'.

If we were asked at random to place it, about whom should we say that the following piece of narrative was written? 'When he had said this, and had taken bread, he gave thanks to God in the presence of all: and he brake it' and began to eat, (Acts 27$^{35-6}$). It is about Paul on board ship in the storm on his way to his next rendezvous with his enemies. With the Master's own Spirit under suffering so manifest in His servant, it was no wonder that they were all of good cheer and themselves also took food.

'*In the night in which he was betrayed, he took bread*' *and gave thanks* (1 Cor 11^{23}).

CHAPTER TEN

My Manner of Life

Thou hast fully known my . . . manner of life (2 Tim 3¹⁰)
Let your manner of life be worthy of the gospel of
Christ (Phil 1²⁷)

THE BIBLE would never have been a complete and sufficient
guide without the life and writings of St Paul. 'His witness',
says Dr Anderson Scott, 'is indispensable to a true understanding and estimate of the Person of Jesus, in the sense that
no interpretation of Jesus can be even remotely satisfactory
which stops short with the Gospels and fails to do justice to
the witness of Paul.' For one thing, we should have been left
with the question: But how does it all work out? There might
even have been the great, pragmatic query: Does it work at
all? The Old Testament had given the Law of God to the
people of God. The weakness was not in the Law, but in
human nature. The prophets pleaded: 'You must worship the
Lord in works as well as words; you must mean what you
pray.' The pause of four centuries between Malachi and
Matthew leaves us wondering how men are ever going to be
able to do what they ought. Not even the Wisdom literature
between the Testaments supplies this gap. So much of it is
escapist. The Wisdom writers are full of high aspirations.
How lovely it will be when the Day of the Lord is come!
If we go on to say that Jesus supplies all that we need because
He is the one prophet who perfectly practises what He
preaches and is able to say not only 'Do what I say', but
'Do what I do', there is also at the back of our mind the hesita-
tion that He is *different*. We are left asking how God's will
can be worked out in the life of a frail-fleshed, strong-willed
human being. This gap is supplied by the writings and lives
of the apostles. The whole theme of fulfilling the righteousness

of God is opened up in Paul's epistles and by his life he interprets to us a way of living which is expressive of the Gospel.

Paul was a Christian. It was when he and Barnabas were working at Antioch that the followers of Jesus were first given that title: '*Christites*.' Among other things it meant that they were *believing in Christ*. All their beliefs, their view of life, their standards and hopes were centred in Jesus. They were *behaving like Christ*. Their all-sufficient pattern was Jesus, and they were seen in the eyes of men to have the characteristics of their Master. (As we shall see, this had come about by way of adoration more than by emulation.) And they were *belonging to Christ*, in the sense that their Christian faith and practice involved a personal allegiance to Jesus Himself and also to their fellow Christians.

But before Paul arrived at this satisfying (not self-satisfied) way of life, he had had a long struggle through youth and early manhood in which he had tried to make ideals come true in his own life. He had tried and failed to translate God's 'Thou shalt' into his own 'I can'. The beginning of this struggle was for him, as for any of his contemporary Jewish friends, a devout enslavement to the Law. This enslavement was in the nature of a passionate attachment which had elements of real affection in it. Those who were Israelites indeed loved their Law and looked on it as the rod and staff of the Good Shepherd. When we read through the Psalms we are left with very many questions unanswered (for instance, particularly concerning the prosperity of the ungodly and the suffering of the righteous), but one fact is never in doubt, that 'the Law of the Lord is perfect, restoring the soul . . . enlightening the eyes' (Ps 19[7, 8]). It was God's gift to Israel as a priceless legacy. For love of His children the Father had opened up His mind to them, and he had said: 'Thou shalt' and 'Thou shalt not' because He cared for them. An obedient child in a Jewish home would look upon the Lord's discipline as part of the security of the everlasting arms and therefore his main source of safety in life.

But what happens when we find ourselves inadequate to fulfil what is expected of us? If we are spineless and vague we may well comfort ourselves by saying: 'One can only do one's best, and after all there are a lot worse than I.' If we are logical and honest, like St Paul or Martin Luther or John Wesley, we shall cry 'Woe is me! Who shall deliver me? I cannot do what I should; I do what I ought not to do.'

Christ met St Paul at the point where his life was in a feverish tension of self-justification and self-despair. In the midst of his persecuting excursions, it is probable that he was in a mood of conscientious passion on behalf of the Law of God. Mingled with that mood was the subconscious knowledge that he himself had failed. All that he says in Romans chapters 1 and 3, as well as in 7 and 8, may well have been his own secret self-criticism. 'Wherein thou judgest another, thou condemnest thyself' (Rom 2¹). It was not that the Law had failed; it was he who had failed to keep the Law. He had been proclaiming the Law as though it were a Gospel. Now he knew that it was only a tutor to lead him to Christ. 'All have sinned, and fall short of the glory of God' (Rom 3²³). However much his mind had tried to serve the Law of the Lord, his flesh had in fact served the dictates of sin (Rom 7²⁵). His manner of life was not worthy of his ideals, because it was based on the slavish obedience to a Law and not filial trust in a Gospel.

The struggle to fulfil all righteousness appears in many forms in human life. A man, for example, longs to be a gentleman. How shall he go about it? One lunch-hour, in a second-hand book shop, he furtively buys a complete *Guide to Etiquette*. This is wonderful, he thinks, so clear and so convincing. He is given guidance on every detail of personal and social life. His mentor (with, in all probability, a double-barrelled name) gives him helpful, brotherly guidance for his life from the rising of the sun to the going down of the same. There may be even a few points added for what goes on in between the going down of the sun and the rising of the same. He sets about his task with a will, knowing that his sweetheart is going to expect great things of him when she takes him to meet her family. But what goes wrong? It is not that any of the commandments and prohibitions in the book are mistaken. They may well be wise and necessary. The plain fact is that a gentleman cannot be produced that way. A gentleman is one from within, or he is no gentleman at all. He would probably do better to spend a day in the company of one man with good manners than to read through all the encyclopedias of etiquette. He may conscientiously try to observe all that the books say, but good manners spring from something far deeper than a quick reference to the textbook for a hint on how to behave in any given situation. If he attains his goal of being a gentleman, he will keep 'the laws of etiquette', but his manners will be acts of grace.

Those who are in Christ are not absolved from the ordinances of the Law. The Law of God remains. Not one jot or tittle of the true Law is to be thrown away. (Though as we remembered earlier, this does not apply to what Jesus called 'the traditions of men'.) The Law still stands for those who have the mind of Christ. In a sense, the Law was a foretaste of the righteousness of Christ. Israel had already had a sip of the living water. 'I mean, they all drank from the supernatural rock that accompanied their travels—and that rock was Christ' (1 Cor 10[4], *NEB*). Jesus goes so far as to tell the rich young ruler that if he could keep the Commandments he would have eternal life. The Christian no more wishes to throw away the original ordinances of God than the graduate scientist would throw away his twice-times table. But how to become a graduate?—that is the problem. How to turn defeat into victory? 'Thanks be to God, which giveth us the victory through our Lord Jesus Christ' (1 Cor 15[57]). To follow the Law as our only hope is a living death. To accept Christ as our only Saviour is a dying life, but it is life indeed.

Now let us follow the process whereby a Christian is enabled to live a manner of life worthy of the gospel.

First of all, it is *of grace, not self-help*. All truly Christian behaviour is based on the fact that God helps us to do what He bids us do. The Law was a gift of God's grace, but that grace was only fully known when the God of love in person came to bring the love which was needful for us if we were to fulfil the Law's demands. This grace of God is manifold in its workings. It is the grace of God which leads us to repent of our failure to keep the Law. It is the grace of God which frees us from that despair which is produced by repentance. 'There is therefore now no condemnation to them that are in Christ Jesus' (Rom 8[1]). It is the grace of God which bridges the gap between our struggling efforts and our dreams of holiness, since in a sense His kindness takes the will for the deed. He is willing to count us as righteous because He sees us with the love that hopeth all things. It is the grace of God that covers the multitude of our sins and attributes to us, for Christ's sake, righteousness not our own.

Did all this mean that Paul settled down to a life-principle that if you do your best, God will see your failures through rose-coloured spectacles? God forbid! Without any shadow of doubt, after his conversion, Paul was more of a perfectionist than before. He saw a depth of righteousness which had never been possible to him in all his study at the feet of Gamaliel. The grace of our Lord Jesus Christ had awakened in him a hunger for righteousness, a passion for gracious living in the true meaning of the term, which he had never known before.

So the next factor is this: that the grace of God had called forth from Paul a response of *gratitude*. 'O to grace how great a debtor, daily I'm constrained to be!' In the Continental statements of Christian faith and practice, it is a common thing for there to be a line drawn under the first section on theology and then for the section on ethics or Christian behaviour to be headed 'Gratitude'. This is meant to imply that the whole of life for a Christian is intended to be an act of gratitude in response to the goodness of God. If God is like *this* . . . we ought to be like *this*. Here we see one of the most notable features of St Paul's epistles. After long sections on the nature of God's redeeming grace, he comes out with a

firm 'Therefore, beloved . . . '. Dr Luke Wiseman used to
tell of a minister who visited an old Christian. He found this
simple half-literate man studying one of the heavier sections of
Paul's letters. The minister said: 'But surely you can't
understand all that solid stuff?' The man replied: 'Well, I
goes on till I comes to a "therefore", then I gets my blessing!'
Many of us know the sense of relief which comes over a congregation when in reading from the epistles we pass from the
grandiloquent theology to the practical ethics.

The point to be remembered is that the 'therefore' is only
the pivot between two ideas. 'Because of this . . . therefore
that'. Our message is always unbalanced and no better than
another exposition of Law if it is only a matter of saying:
'Put on love', without stating the motive. Our full message is:
Christ loved us and gave Himself for us, therefore we ought to
love one another. In the Communion Service, when we read
the Commandments of our Lord Jesus, three are given:
'Love God', 'love your neighbour as yourself', and then a
third. This sounds repetitive, but it is nothing of the kind.
The third Commandment says that we are to 'love one another
as Christ loved us'. This constitutes the uniqueness of Christianity. So for St Paul, Christian behaviour is based not
so much on what we ought to do, but on what Christ has done
for us. Paul did not urge the people of Antioch to continue
trying to be good Christians. He urged them to continue in
the grace of God. We are to walk worthily of the Gospel. We
are to receive one another, as Christ received us. We are to
forgive as we have been forgiven.

Let us go a step farther: Suppose a man responds to the
grace of God in Christ? Suppose grace has called forth a passion to live a gracious life? How does the stamp of Christ's
nature come upon his character? By what process does a
Christian become Christlike? It is not enough for us to say
that we ought to be like Him, for that is only to exchange one
'ought' for another. Many of the terms we have used since
childhood imply a type of discipleship which the critics of
Christianity might well dismiss as little more than devout

aspirations, if we do not explain their meaning clearly. 'To follow Jesus', for example, has never seemed to me an adequate translation of a word which means 'to go along in company with'. Similarly, the classic phrase 'The Imitation of Christ' would at first sight suggest a process of copying Jesus religiously. But a dutiful life which is beset with the self-conscious question: 'What would Jesus do?' has very little spontaneity or naturalness about it. Yet it is somewhere here that the secret lies. 'Be ye imitators of me, even as I also am of Christ' (1 Cor 11[1]), says Paul to the Corinthians, using a word that actually implies mimicry. This is really the same thought as that in the Letter to the Hebrews, where the writer speaks of 'looking unto Jesus, the author and perfector, of our faith'. Jesus is also the perfector of our practice, and 'looking unto Him' is the secret of the Christian's manner of life.

This impact of Jesus Christ upon the believer is best understood if we think in terms of personal influence *unselfconsciously* received. Take for instance, the impression made by a nanny on a child during those years when a child quietly absorbs impressions without much self-analysis and by a simple process of companionship and observation. For good or ill, the child takes over something of the woman's character. (One marvels at the ease with which some middle-class parents will leave their child in the care of another for twenty hours or more in a day.) I knew of one nanny who had a stooping shoulder, and before very long the child in her care developed the same stoop. By conscious imitation? No, not at all. She was a natural mimic, and without thought she behaved like one whom she loved. In later years when she married a minister and travelled in various parts of England, her family found that within a matter of a few weeks, she was picking up the lilt and idiom of the local dialect. This was not a matter of mocking at the yokels. It was far more a process of affectionate concentration. As she lived with people, she became like them. I knew another child who had a Scottish nanny, and when his mother one day found him in great distress, anxious because he thought she had left him alone in the house, he said in tears:

'I thocht ye were awa'!' The child was quite unaware of having deviated from his parents' standard English!

The element of graciousness in the life of a Christian is the result of direct contact with the grace of our Lord Jesus Christ. But it is not there through any self-conscious means. When Moses had been gazing into the unseen, to catch a glimpse of the Lord Jehovah, he came down from the mountain with his face radiant. He was transfigured. But we are expressly told that 'he wist not that the skin of his face shone' (Ex 34[29]). It was not that he thought he had better look as though he had had a wonderful spiritual experience because this would impress the waiting crowd! His face was transfigured without his knowing it.

In Psalm 34[5]: 'They looked unto Him and were lightened.' 'Thou shalt see and be lightened', says Isaiah (Isa 60[5]). This is very different from saying, 'Look unto Him and then generate some electricity of your own.'

Or, to think in terms of hearing, rather than seeing, it is for us to use the 'inward ear' to hear our Master's voice. What we hear in the ear will be manifest to men in the street, as well as on the housetops.

> *And beauty born of murmuring sound*
> *Shall pass into her face. . . .*

I stood one winter's night at a bus stop. In the building across the road, some dancers were moving rhythmically around in a dance-hall in the upstairs room. The windows were shut, but the curtains were open. I could hear no music, but it was obvious that they were in unison together because they were under the control of music audible to each of them. It is not only our personal life but also our life together as Christians which lets the world see that we have a Master in heaven.

> *Hence may all our actions flow,*
> *Love the proof that Christ we know;*
> *Mutual love the token be,*
> *Lord, that we belong to Thee.*

It is here that the experts in the life of *worship* have so much to tell us. I am not thinking of those who are only concerned with the gymnastics of worship; I am referring to those who know that the most important thing in life is the vision of God in the face of Jesus Christ. Such spiritual guides always emphasize that the worshipper is only fully worshipping when his whole mind is turned away from himself toward God. This beatific vision will make an impression on his life which will issue in goodness of character.

Unfortunately, it is possible to do a lot of contemplating without its making an impression on our manner of life; as George Eliot said, there are 'people whose celestial intimacies do not seem to have improved their domestic manners'. But the relationship is indispensable. Looking unto Jesus we are perfected, as the Holy Spirit, which is His Spirit, fills our lives without our worrying too much about what is happening to us.

Unless we are very vain we do not go away on holiday merely to acquire a sun-browned face. When we return home, our friends may well say: 'I can see that you've been in the sun all right.' Our inward health shows itself in our countenance. So, on the highest plane, the Christian knows that Christ is in him, when men see his manner of life and take knowledge of him that he has been with Jesus.

Upon the whole life of a Christian there will be one predominating mark and that is love. Love is the life of God, and if we draw near to Him who has drawn near to us, it will be love that pervades all thought and action.

'When the evening of your life comes', says St John of the Cross, 'you will be judged on love.' It is for this reason we shall be judged by God, and God is love.

CHAPTER ELEVEN

My Neighbour

Speak ye truth each one with his neighbour, for we are
members one of another (Eph 4[25])

TO BE taking one's temperature as a frequent habit is usually
a sign of an unhealthy mind as well as of an unhealthy con-
stitution. Yet one cannot dispense with a thermometer either
physically or spiritually. There are times when self-examina-
tion is necessary. Whilst it is better to spend hours of medita-
tion remembering how much God loves us ('Ten looks at
Christ for every one at self'), it is right at least to spend
minutes asking: 'How much do I love God?'

The New Testament has a simple measuring gauge for test-
ing our love for God, and it is this: How much do I love my
neighbour? 'He that loveth not his brother whom he hath
seen', says John, 'cannot love God whom he hath not seen'
(1 John 4[20]). 'This commandment have we from him—that he
who loveth God love his brother also.' If the love of God is
shed abroad in our hearts, we shall not need to be told to love
our brother. 'Concerning love of the brethren', says Paul to
the Thessalonians, 'ye have no need that one write unto you:
for ye yourselves are taught of God to love one another'
(1 Thess 4[9]).

There is no such thing as Christianity in a vacuum. All
Christian virtues involve relationships, and to have the mind
of Christ means that one is even more involved in personal
ties than the natural man. We should find it very hard to keep
our Christianity alive on a desert island. It might be a good
plan to take with us some discs of congregational singing, or a
selection of human voices and the sounds of city streets or
of a factory workshop in order to keep contact with human
fellowship.

It must be desperately hard to be a Christian in solitary confinement with only a warder on whom to lavish the sacrament of service without which the Christian character languishes. Perhaps that is why Paul appears to have spent so much of his time in prison writing letters. He was able to draw into the four walls of his cell the care of the Churches. In the darkness of his prison he was able to be a light to them that were in the darkness of unbelief. One suspects that his warders were soon bound to him not only by ankle chains but also by his persistent concern for their welfare. 'One soul is diocese enough for a Bishop,' said Cardinal Manning, and if at times St Paul had only a Roman centurion as neighbour, he would find in him the necessary quorum for the exercise of love which always needs someone to be loved. The very doctrine of the Trinity points to the nature of God as loving and loved. The doctrine of creation should always include the thought that God made man because He wanted to love him, and we are all made in God's image.

From our birth we are a member in a small unit of society. To be a human being, let alone a Christian, involves taking up an attitude to those who share the stuff of life with us. We may, of course, rebel against the demands of human relationship. There are some who seem early in life to decide that they will limit their ship's company for the voyage of life and live as though those whom they have not taken aboard do not exist. But to do this is to renounce for ever the mind of Christ, who told us that even a man who happened to be lying by the roadside was still our neighbour. So long as we go on through life asking: 'But who is my neighbour?' we are in effect asking: 'Where can I limit the demands of human society upon me? What are the minimum requirements?' Once and for all Christ has established the principle that on the basis of one blood in creation, and one blood in redemption, all men are our neighbours, and to live is to live in company. We may as well reconcile ourselves to this, even if we pride ourselves on being of a reserved introversial temperament. We may find life difficult with father and with our prodigal

younger brother; we may use the servants of this world
merely to inquire what is happening; we may resent the
neighbours coming in, with their music and dancing; but this
is life. There is always someone else in the household besides
us, and if one day we want to be fit company for angels and
archangels and all the company of Heaven, we may as well
learn to live with folk.

How then is the Christian to treat his neighbour? There is
a phrase which at first glance sounds transparently Christian:
'He treats everyone alike.' It conjures up the picture of a good
straightforward man with no snobbery, no respect of persons,
no unworthy prejudices. He treats everyone alike, peer and
peasant; they are all the same to him. But it only takes a
quick second glance to see how shallow and inadequate this
assessment is. To treat people all the same way is tantamount
to treating them as though they *are* all the same, and this is
simply not true. In actual fact, if I treat everyone alike, it will
involve my reducing personal relationships to a type of im-
personal electric current. It will almost certainly mean that
my association is at a superficial level only. I may hand out a
cup of tea from the same teapot and give a biscuit from the
same tin to a company of people, but to have a friendship
with each one of them is a very different matter. Jesus loved
Martha and Mary and Lazarus, but His bond with them was
different in each case. One could never say that Jesus treated
everyone alike. Each man was a man in his own right, and
love is, above all things, personal and individual. When Paul
said he was all things to all men, his whole point was that he
gave himself entirely to each man according to each man's
need. He treated a Jew as a Jew, and a Gentile as a Gentile.

This shallow conception of human relationships is sometimes seen in the wrong ideas people have about justice. The
courts of our land do not dispense the same fines and damages
to everyone, even on charges which to a layman look identical.
But this is not justice! we may say. The judges know better
and will assess damages according to a man's ability to pay and
according to the effect the case has had on his reputation or

livelihood. The punishment must not only fit the crime, it must also fit the criminal. Similarly, in the world of education, a teacher is by many people considered 'fair' if he or she 'treats every child exactly alike'. Children, fortunately, have more wisdom; they know deep down in their young hearts whether or not their teacher is basically just. They will trust him far more if he has the courage to treat each pupil as a person, rather than if he runs the class as so many car-tyres that need equal pressure.

Nevertheless, this takes character and courage. When my grandfather was Principal of Southlands Training College for Women, they used to tease him, and love him, for saying to a student who asked a favour: 'Well, Miss So-and-so, you can do for one what you can't do for a hundred and twenty-nine'. It takes a very good disciplinarian to behave in that way. A more timorous head is always saying: 'If I do it for one, I shall have to do it for a hundred and twenty-nine.'

God loves us all as though we were each His only child, even though it is never our business to behave as though we were. He has set His love upon us as upon someone who is different from anyone else in the world, because we *are* different. The palmists as well as the psalmists know that! No two of us are the same, even though we may be similar, and even though we may all need the same Saviour. So when I come to consider my neighbour, I must above all remember that he is a unique person. He is not only different from me, he is different from all my other neighbours. However much our sentiment may like to stress the equality of all men, the fact stands, that all men are not the same, either in relationship to God or to us.

Herein lies a corrective to a terrible flaw in the modern scheme of things. Far too often we decide on certain conveni- ent groupings of society and go on to assume that people within those groups are identical. 'The whites.' 'The blacks.' 'The workers.' 'The Germans.' Is there no difference between a Christian German and a Nazi German? And were all Nazi Germans as alike as their jackboots made them appear to be?

So it comes about that, in the rich pattern of our life, it is demanded of us that we are confronted with a new experience of fellowship and a new challenge every time we meet a fellow pilgrim on the road. 'We are the sum of the people we have met', and our characters are formed by this constant process of adjustment in our personal relationship. In a sense we need to change our wavelength for each transmission.

We are now ready to deal with a factor that has to be reckoned with in our Christian behaviour. There is no escape from the division of human beings into those who are *within* the fold and those who are *without*. Under these two heads we have an infinite variety of neighbours—but we cannot avoid the fact that they are in different neighbourhoods. This sounds thoroughly unchristian, a form of exclusiveness and pride such as darkens the history of Israel. Were not the children of Israel guilty of a type of tribal isolationism which counted the Gentile as outside the pale? And has not Jesus broken down the middle wall of partition? But let us wait a moment; Jesus has never led us to believe that there is no difference between those who have been gathered into His fold and those who have not. We must not glide off into nebulous talk about 'lots of good in the worst of us'. Those who say that there is no great difference between a Christian and a non-Christian always prove themselves within a few sentences to have a very hazy idea of what it means to be a Christian. The difference between 'knowing Christ' and not knowing Him is the difference between darkness and light. 'He that hath the Son hath the life and he that hath not the Son of God hath not the life.' If we are to enter fully into Christ's mind on this matter we shall need more of Paul's honest realism than we are accustomed to show.

Let it be said categorically that, according to Jesus, a Christian's neighbours include both those who are within and those who are without. We are not talking now about which is the best denomination for those who want to be sure that they are inside! But we are saying that the Lord knoweth them that are His, and that it is sentimental and unreal to pretend that there is not a special type of neighbourliness involved for those who have responded to the call of Christ.

Paul was in no doubt about all this. His love soon surmounted any rigid division of Jew versus Gentile, but he was so sure of the change that Christ had wrought in his soul, that he knew that to be in Christ was to be a new creation and honesty demanded that he should admit that the friends of Jesus were in a class of their own. As we shall see in a moment, his previous error in Judaism checked him from an attitude of superior scorn towards the unbeliever. But if we know what it is to have Christ, and in Him to have all things, we cannot for one moment baulk this issue, that to be without Christ is an even more pitiable condition than to be alienated from the commonwealth of Israel.

The implications of all this are fraught with dangers, but let us grasp the nettle boldly. Let us now see the mind of Christ worked out in Paul in relation, first, to those within the new covenant, and then in relation to those without.

THOSE WHO ARE WITHIN

From time to time it appears that Jesus was overheard murmuring His prayers half aloud (an excellent practice, incidentally, for us as an aid to concentration). In these moments of deep intimacy it is clear that He was aware of a new society, a new class if you will, growing up around Him. 'Those whom Thou hast given Me out of the world' is a perfect description of the new Israel. His first converts little realized that they were the beginning of a new creation. He had started to draw all men to Himself and the beginning of the process was seen in that small band of diverse men who had responded to His call. It would appear that even within this band there were degrees of intimacy—the seventy; the twelve; Peter, James and John; the Beloved Disciple. But the main distinction was that there were those who were following and those who were not. Is it surprising that Jesus found a special joy in the company of those who were with Him, which He could not be expected to find with those who were against Him?

As we read the gospels can we not see a friendship being forged between Jesus and His disciples, which is not the same as His friendship with tax-gatherers and sinners. It was with those who had continued with Him in His temptations that He longed to eat the passover before He suffered (Lk 22¹⁵). He does not hesitate to call them apart as a separate group and in so doing He made them marked men. They were becoming a sect of the Nazarene. It is no good hitting our heads against a wall on this matter. Either we join Jesus outside the camp, or we don't. 'He that is not for Me is against Me.' When once a man had said, 'All right, Jesus, I'll come,' he could never be the same again without being a traitor. We see that band of brothers, those few, those happy few, gathering together to Jesus to tell Him all things. Here was a new neighbourhood. It was the beginning of the City of God coming down from heaven. To belong to Christ was to be in a society that was to be the leaven of the world, 'the soul of the world' in fact, and a neighbour within that society was a special person indeed.

> *Inseparably joined in heart*
> *The friends of Jesus are.*

Now St Paul is imbued with this sense of belonging to a special company. He and his fellow-Christians had been united by God's grace, and this implied a bond so close that it was like nothing else on earth. It was the life-work of St Paul to perfect the bond of neighbourliness between the fellow members of Christ's Church so that the world might see how the Christians loved one another. The very blue-print for the perfect society must be manifest in each fellowship, or society, as we Methodists call it. How often the man of the world can look over the churchyard wall, like Chad in the funny little cartoon of war-time, and say: 'Wot, no charity?' Paul yearned over the Churches as Christ yearned over his band of apostles. He wanted the world to know that God had sent Jesus, and how else could they know except by the Church's being completely one in Him? It would make an interesting study to compare John the Baptist, who presented the Lamb of God to the world, and St Paul, who presented the Church to the world. It was to Paul more than any one single servant of God that we owe the fact that by the end of the first century a pagan was able to write of the Christians: 'This is a new people!'

> Our friendship sanctify and guide:
> Unmixed with selfishness and pride,
>   Thy glory be our single aim!
> In all our intercourse below,
> Still let us in Thy footsteps go,
>   And never meet but in Thy Name.
>
> Whate'er thou dost on one bestow,
> Let each the double blessing know;
>   Let each the common burden bear;
> In comforts and in griefs agree;
> And wrestle for his friends with thee,
>   In all the omnipotence of prayer.

For St Paul, belonging to the Church involves the putting of certain claims first. The Christian is to 'work that which is good toward all men, and especially toward them that are of the household of the faith' (Gal 6¹⁰). 'If any provideth not for his own, and especially his own household, he hath denied the faith, and is worse than an unbeliever' (1 Tim 5⁸). The members of Christ's body must never forget that their standard of behaviour is to be perfection. There is reason to believe that Philippians 2, verse 5, is best interpreted as: 'Have this mind among yourselves in your treatment of one another which was also in Christ Jesus.' All disputes must be settled within the family. Dare any of you, having a matter against his (Christian) neighbour, go to law before the unrighteous, and not before the saints? (1 Cor 6¹). Has not the Master said: 'If thy brother sin against thee, go, shew him his fault between thee and him alone'? (Mt 18¹⁵). Trial before a pagan court must always be a Christian's last resort in dealing with a fellow Christian. 'What have I to do with judging them that are without?' Paul asks the Corinthians.

'Do not ye judge them that are within, whereas them that are without God judgeth?' (1 Cor 5¹²⁻¹³). 'It is altogether a defect in you, that ye have lawsuits one with another' (1 Cor 6⁷). In all things a Christian should 'walk in wisdom toward them that are without, redeeming the time' (Col 4⁵).

> *Jesus, Thou precious corner-stone,*
> *Preserve inseparably one*
> * Whom Thou didst by Thy Spirit join:*
> *Still let us in Thy Spirit live,*
> *And to Thy church the pattern give*
> * Of unanimity divine.*

There is one particular sin in a Christian fellowship about which St Paul spoke with the same horror as his Master, and that is the desire to have the first place. Our Lord was quick to sense, as He walked along the road to Jerusalem ahead of His disciples that all was not wholesome in their conversation. It was the familiar sin of place-seeking, as familiar now as then. Who should be first? Who should have the left and right seat at the Messianic banquet? Whenever we detect such things in the life of the Church we are right to remind one another that we simply don't do things like that in a Christian fellowship. However much the Gentiles lord it over one another, the only top people in the household of the faith are those who serve, those who are least, those who have the spirit of the child (Mk 10⁴²⁻⁴⁵).

So St Paul bade his fellow Christians to prefer one another in honour (Rom 12¹⁰). Had not the Master said: 'If I then, your Lord and Master, have washed your feet, ye also ought to wash one another's feet'? (Jn 13¹⁴.) In lowliness of mind they were to count each one better than himself (Phil 2³). They were to subject themselves to one another in the fear of Christ' (Eph 5²¹). God's elect must 'put on a heart of humility, meekness' (Col 3¹²). All this meekness is the reflection of the mind of Christ who is the Lamb of God (2 Cor 10¹).

THOSE WHO ARE WITHOUT

St Paul followed in the steps of a Saviour who had been the Good Samaritan of the human race. Charles Wesley, in his paraphrase of the parable, cries:

> *Saviour of my soul, draw nigh,*
> *In mercy haste to me;*
> *At the point of death I lie,*
> *And cannot come to thee.*

This fact of Christ's having drawn near to sinners was an all-sufficient reason for Paul's drawing near and keeping near his neighbour in the world, whoever he might be. Calvary had shattered all his exclusiveness. The Friend of Sinners had made Paul a friend even of barbarians. He had no false humility or spurious sentiment that 'we are all very much the same when you get under the surface'. When you got under the surface of Paul you found Christ. When you got under the surface of the unbeliever you found that 'his senseless heart was darkened' (Rom 1²¹).

In Paul's epistles you will find the familiar analogies of Jesus to imply that the disciple is in the world not to be over-come of evil but to overcome evil with good. There is no question of the Christian's getting covered with tar because he touches pitch. Jesus says we are the leaven who alter the shape of things to come (Mt 13³³). So also says St Paul: 'A little leaven leavens the whole lump. I have confidence to you-ward' (Gal 5⁹⁻¹⁰). Jesus says: 'Ye are the light of the world' (Mt 5¹⁴). St Paul says to the Thessalonians: 'Ye are all sons of light, and sons of the day' (1 Thess 5⁵), and to the Ephesians: 'Ye were once darkness, but are now light in the Lord: walk as children of light' (Eph 5⁸). They are to have no fellowship with the unfruitful works of darkness, but rather reprove them (verse 11). But then Jesus had always said that light rebukes darkness: 'Every one that doeth ill hateth the light' (Jn 3²⁰). The point is that light shines out *into* the darkness; the little candle is right in the midst of a naughty world. Jesus says that we are 'the salt of the earth' (Mt 5¹³). St Paul tells us that we are 'a sweet savour of Christ unto God, in them that are being saved, and in them that are perishing' (2 Cor 2[15]). Our very speech must be 'seasoned with salt' (Col 4[6]).

The common factor in all these analogies is that the Christian is near enough to his brother to influence him, and he must do so and not allow himself to be contaminated by evil. Paul is well aware of this danger: 'Be not deceived: Evil company doth corrupt good manners' (1 Cor 15[33]). Satan desires to have Simon Peter, and a disciple is liable to fall away under the world's influence. 'Help! Come quickly', Paul cries to Timothy; 'Demas has fallen in love with this world.' As the little girl said: 'Mummy says little girls are too much like apples; bad apples make good apples bad before good apples make bad apples good!' The Christian must be in the world but not of the world. Both Jesus and Paul would have approved the illustration of Sadhu Sundar Singh: 'The Christian is like a boat. The boat must be in the water, but the water must not be in the boat.'

Paul had forsaken once for all the hedged-in world of Pharisaism; and he was out and about in the world. 'I cannot praise', says Milton, 'a fugitive and cloistered virtue, un-exercised and unbreathed, that never sallies out and sees her adversary but shrinks out of the race, when that immortal garland is to be run for not without dust and heat.' And Robert Louis Stevenson adds: 'There is apt to be something unmanly, something almost dastardly, in a life that does not move with dash and freedom and that fears the bracing contact of the world.' 'It is better', says William James, 'that a life should contract many a dustmark than forfeit usefulness in its effort to remain unspotted.'

Let us now examine briefly Paul's example and guidance in our relationship with our neighbour in the world, and we shall see how Christlike it all is.

(1) Those in Authority Over Us

The Kingdom to which we belong is not of this world (Jn 18[36]). We are citizens of the heavenly Kingdom and our stay in the world is as ambassadors in residence, due any time to be called home (Phil 3²⁰). But so long as we are here, we are to claim full rights of citizenship and accept full duties of citizenship in the empire of this world.

Pilate would have had no power if it had not been given to him by God. 'There is no power but of God', said Paul; 'The powers that be are ordained of God' (Rom 13¹). For this reason we shall both fear them, and yet not be afraid of them. Paul accepted the rebuke when he discovered that he had been insulting a High Priest and quoted Exodus 22, verse 28: 'Thou shalt not curse a ruler of thy people'. The Master accepted with dignity the indignity of being bound in front of a Roman Governor. Pilate was doing what he had been appointed to do, and for Jesus to allow Himself to appear before him made no concession whatsoever to the injustice of the trial. Jesus gave as His guiding dictum: 'Render unto Caesar that which is Caesar's'; so, said Paul, 'Render to all their dues: tribute to whom tribute is due, custom to whom custom, fear to whom fear, honour to whom honour' (Rom 13⁷). Christian citizenship involves being loyal to the body politic. You are not more Christlike for being an awkward cuss. Did not Jesus our Master pay the half-shekel? It was a totally untrue charge that they had found Jesus perverting the nation and forbidding to give tribute to Caesar (Mt 17²⁴, Lk 23²).

Similarly, in the sphere of employment, the Christian sees no indignity in serving a master. Whether or not Jesus was ever apprenticed to Joseph we do not know. But He was certainly employed by the public, and the man who paid the carpenter would call the tune about the size and shape of a yoke. The dignity of service has once for all been established by Jesus. When a London bus conductress was reminded that she was a servant of the public she replied in horror: 'Me, a servant! I'm nobody's servant!' But a Christian is ready to follow St Paul: 'Servants, be obedient unto them that according to the flesh are your masters, with fear and trembling, in singleness of heart, as unto Christ' (Eph 6⁵). That is the point; the 'Inasmuch' of the parable of the sheep and the goats

applies in relation to our foreman, shop-steward, superinten-
dent, department manager, as much as it does to a Hungarian
refugee who has prompted our pity. It may be harder to like
a brother whom we have seen than a brother whom we have
not seen. But whatever we do we must work heartily, as
unto the Lord, not unto men (Col 3²³).

(2) *Those on an Equality with Us*

It is clear from the gospel narrative, that Jesus was a com-
panionable man. His principle did not make Him 'spiky'
in company. Those who did not come to Him with a previously
infected allergy found Him good to be with, and He who has
no equal was a man among men. It must have been a wonderful thing to hear the Saviour of the world call you 'Friend'. It
was music in those sinners' ears when they heard a shout:
'Boys, have you got anything to eat?'

A Christian should be good to live with. Paul had much
to say about the ordinary relationships we have with our
fellows. He loved the sense of comradeship which God has
implanted in us. His references to his brethren, his work-
fellows, his fellow-prisoners, his fellow-slaves, his fellow-
labourers, his dearly beloved, his helpers, would all suggest
that he practised what he preached. As far as in him lay, he
was at peace with all men (Rom 12¹⁸). Montefiore says: 'The
principle of not giving needless offence is used with great insight
and power by Paul.' Jesus had said: 'Have salt in yourselves and
be at peace with one another' (Mk 9⁵⁰). Whatever his appearance, and however sternly he may have spoken and written from
time to time, Paul must have been good company. We miss a
great deal in our reading of St Paul if we hold the mistaken
idea that he was an angular little man, always at cross purposes
with his neighbours. His speech would have grace as well as
salt (Col 4⁶). He believed that the peace of Christ ought to rule a
man's heart, and the word of Christ should dwell in him richly
(Col 3¹⁵⁻¹⁶). A Christian is one who has turned and become a
little child, and though wise as a serpent he should be harmless
as a dove (Mt 10¹⁶). So even though in mind, said Paul, he is

to be a man, in malice he must be a babe. We ought to follow
after the things which make for peace, and things whereby we
may edify one another.

There is an admirable short summary of St Paul's teaching
about human conduct in Dr Anderson Scott's *St Paul, the
Man and the Teacher*. He reminds us that Paul stressed that
we must do what is expedient, what is fitting or becoming.
We must be considerate. We must not claim our rights up to
the hilt. All this is Christlike behaviour. A man who pursues
such a course will prove himself a good friend to his fellows.

(3) *Those Under Our Authority*

You can tell a gentleman by the way he treats a waitress.
The great contribution of the uniformed organizations among
young people has been that they have been taught both the
giving and the taking of orders. Many forget that both lessons
have to be learned in life, and they think of Scouting and
Guiding, for instance, as useful ways for boys and girls to
learn obedience. But they also teach the discipline of being a
leader. To give orders is no simple undertaking, and the
modern world badly needs men who know how to be a boss
without being bossy.

Jesus does not say much about the theory of management.
Quite simply He tells us that He has given us an example as our
Lord and Master. When the Burma surgeon wanted to teach
the local nurses not to be too proud to get down to digging
drains, the only way he could do it was by himself taking up a
spade. Perhaps there is no sphere of behaviour where Christ
is more of a challenge to our times than when He says that
leaders must be slaves (Mk 10⁴⁴).

Paul is an echo of this injunction when he tells masters that
they are to treat their servants as their servants are to treat
them. 'Ye masters, do the same things unto them, and forbear
threatening' (Eph 6⁹). 'Masters, render unto your servants
that which is just and equal' (Col 4¹). Above all, he begs them
not to forget that they have a master in Heaven.

Christianity also had something fresh to say about how we

I

are to treat those who are at our mercy. It would not be true
to say that it introduced an entirely new thought to the world in
making a virtue of compassion; magnanimity, large-hearted-
ness, the exercise of self-control in the handling of men in
your power—these were virtues recognized by the Romans.
But to show pity was looked upon as a rare phenomenon.
The normal behaviour of a conqueror was to be ruthless. To
be strong implied the capacity to behave victoriously, and the
common man's concept of a victor was a general on horse-
back leading a chain of captive slaves. But Jesus called all
men to be merciful, even as our heavenly Father is merciful
(Lk 6[36]).

As we read the Acts of the Apostles we can see this grace of
human compassion filtering into the life of the world. Where
is there a parallel in the pagan literature of the first century
with the collection made by the disciples, every man according
to his ability, for the famine victims in Judea (Acts 11[28-9])?
A new convert in the Philippian gaol washes the stripes of
those who were really his victims (Acts 16[33]). St Paul presses
home this spirit of Christian magnanimity. To friends at
Ephesus he says: 'You ought to help the weak, and to remember
the words of the Lord Jesus, how he himself said, It is more
blessed to give than to receive' (Acts 20[35]). Christ has given
him a special concern for the weak. The weak brother must
not be wounded; the brother overtaken in a trespass is to be
restored (1 Cor 8[12]). If we are to fulfil the law of Christ we
must bear such burdens for another (Gal 6[1-2]).

But perhaps there is no more perfect example of the Christian's duty in relation to his subordinate than in the epistolary
gem to Philemon. I can never understand why people say
there is nothing in the Bible against slavery. A pagan who read
the letter to Philemon must have felt as a jingoist empire
builder felt when he saw Stafford Cripps at work in India:
'If we go on like this, the days of the Empire are over!' If you
start expecting a master to welcome back a runaway slave and
treat him as a brother and fellow Church member, and withal
greet him by saying: 'Your holiday seems to have done us

both good!' you can't expect the good old days of pitiless slavery to last for ever.

(4) *Those in Opposition to Us*

Here again we must be clear not to claim any unmerited originality for Christian standards. There was a high ideal set, for instance, by the writers of the Wisdom literature. The writer of the Proverbs says: 'If thine enemy be hungry, give him bread to eat and if he be thirsty, give him water to drink' (Prov 25[21]). But that applied to those at your mercy. What of the times when you yourself were at their mercy?

The natural man cries with Samson: 'O Lord God strengthen me that I may be avenged on mine enemies.' But this dark and evil spirit has for ever been rebuked by a cry from the Cross, when we hear Jesus pray for His enemies: 'Father, forgive them for they know not what they do.' We hear this cry on our behalf, and it is as a balm for our fear of judgement and as a challenge to our love of revenge.

> *Forgive my foes? it cannot be;*
> *My foes with cordial care embrace?*
> *Fast bound in sin and misery,*
> *Unsaved, unchanged by hallowing grace,*
> *Throughout my fallen soul I feel*
> *With man this is impossible.*
>
> *Root out the wrath thou dost restrain;*
> *And when I have my Saviour's mind,*
> *I cannot render pain for pain,*
> *I cannot speak a word unkind,*
> *An angry thought I cannot know,*
> *Or count mine injurer my foe.*

The intercession for enemies comes down through the ages like a glorious scarlet thread in the tapestry of Christian history, from the first Christian martyr praying in the spirit of his Master, 'Lay not this sin to their charge', down to Bishop Wilson as a prisoner in a Japanese prison camp, praying for his torturers. St Paul, who had been merciless as a persecutor, but who had then seen and heard Stephen die, magnificently caught this Christian grace. 'Bless them that persecute you'; he said, 'bless, and curse not.' 'Render to no man evil for evil'. 'Avenge not yourselves' (Rom 12$^{14, 17, 19}$). 'Why not rather take wrong?' he asked the Corinthians (1 Cor 6^7). The mind of Christ on the mount did indeed indwell him. 'Resist not him that is evil, but whosoever smiteth thee on thy right cheek, turn to him the other also' (Mt 5^{39}).

Those who have the mind of Christ are committed to a hard way indeed—the way of the Cross which demands the grace to cover another's sin.

CHAPTER TWELVE

My Body

Christ shall be magnified in my body (Phil 1[20])

THERE IS only one God. He has only one Kingdom, and everything that He made in that Kingdom is worthy of Him. 'God saw everything that he had made, and, behold, it was very good' (Gen 1[31]). 'All things were made by God', as John says, 'and without him was not anything made that hath been made' (Jn 1[3]). Or, as Paul puts it, 'Of him and through him and unto him are all things' (Rom 11[36]).

And yet one cannot read the Bible without discovering that within the whole scheme of things there are contradictory and contrasting elements. For one thing there is a power of evil in rebellion against God, as well as a power that makes for righteousness. There is also in the Bible a distinction made between 'the things that are seen' and are 'temporal'—and 'the things that are not seen' and are 'eternal'. This is Paul's phraseology. The corresponding distinction is found in the teaching of Jesus, when He speaks about the 'treasures of earth' over against the 'treasures of Heaven', and when He refers to 'the body' in contrast to 'the soul' or 'the life'.

Having discovered this in the Bible, many go on to draw a false conclusion, which may be expressed loosely in the following way—that God has made an inferior type of commodity in the physical world (of which the Christian must see as little as possible) and a far superior article in the spiritual sphere (which is thoroughly respectable and gilt-edged). In other words, they line up in their mind physical-and-evil *versus* spiritual-and-good.

This is not only naïve; it is wrong. For one thing the power of evil is not confined to this world, or to 'flesh and blood', as Paul would say (Eph 6[12]). It is found in 'the spiritual hosts

CHRIST IN ME

of wickedness in the heavenly places'. The fallacy is equally evident when we realize that no Christian can speak disparagingly of things physical when he remembers that his faith is rooted in the fact that God Himself made use of a human body for the salvation of the world. He was 'born of a woman' (Gal 4⁴), 'in the likeness of men' (Phil 2⁷), and He reconciled us 'in the body of his flesh through death' (Col 1²²). The Incarnation of Jesus has for ever given a sanctity to human flesh. It is well to remember this when we feel that our own flesh is too solid, or sullied, and wish that it would melt! Christ's body was an adequate medium for God Almighty. 'In Him dwelleth all the fulness of the Godhead' *in a body* (Col 2⁹). Jesus was able to give us the New Covenant *in His blood.*

This means that we must avoid what is called Dualism—that is, making a complete separation between spirit (as something good) and matter (as something evil). Many have accused Paul of this heresy. Sometimes they stress the point that Paul seems to have had a 'narrow' view of the physical side of marriage, as though everything to do with sex were evil. Sometimes they remind us that Paul does not seem, judging from the absence of nature-notes in his epistles, to have taken into his consideration, as Jesus did, the flowers of the field and the birds of the air. Paul may rightly be charged with not being a nature poet; but after all he was a city dweller and all his journeys through the countryside were for evangelism rather than for sightseeing. But he never cast a slur on anything which God had made.

The real emphasis in Paul lies in the distinction he makes (following the Mind of his Master) between the *temporal* and the *eternal*. He does not, like some later heretical Dualists, fall into the trap of suggesting that there is anything inherently evil in the things of the body. 'Know ye not that your body is a temple of the Holy Ghost which is in you, which ye have from God?' (1 Cor 6¹⁹). (God would not have given us anything *evil*.) 'I know, and am persuaded in the Lord Jesus, that nothing is unclean of itself: save that to him who accounteth anything to be unclean, to him it is unclean' (Rom 14[14]). Had not the Master said—'there is nothing from without the man, that going into him can defile him: but the things which proceed out of the man are those that defile the man'? (Mk 7[15]). What is in the heart may be unclean, but his body is not to be blamed. Jesus is clearly saying that we must not attribute evil to what is amoral.

The important thing to realize is that for Jesus and Paul the material world is *temporary*. 'The things which are seen are temporal, but the things which are not seen are eternal' (2 Cor 4[18]). Our body is a 'tent' or 'tabernacle'. 'The Word was made flesh', says John, 'and dwelt (pitched His tent) among us.' So, says St Paul, 'If the earthly home that houses us today be demolished, we possess a building which God has prepared' (2 Cor 5[1]). Again, he says, 'We have this treasure (of mortal life) in earthen vessels' (2 Cor 4[7]).

> *We know, by faith we know,*
> *   If this vile house of clay,*
> *This tabernacle, sink below*
> *   In ruinous decay,*
> *We have a house above,*
> *   Not made with mortal hands,*
> *And firm, as our Redeemer's love,*
> *   That heavenly fabric stands.*

Our Father has many mansions for our indwelling, and the mansion of the body in which we now dwell is *not made to last*. This last thought is a truism of which the prophets were fully aware. 'All flesh is grass, and all the goodliness thereof is as the flower of the field: the grass withereth, the flower fadeth ... surely the people is grass' (Isa 40[6-7]). Dr Paul S. Sears, writing of 'Deserts on the March', says: 'The face of the earth is a grave-yard, and so it has always been.' Our very skin only lasts as long as a man's winter coat. It is decaying even while we feel in robust health.

Queen Elizabeth, the Queen Mother, visited a certain Home for Incurables in 1938 and again in 1961. It is reported that she met one patient who was still in the hospital when she went on the second occasion. 'Incurable' for twenty-three years! But we are *all* incurable! We all have a fatal skin disease. Man, you're dying! I can see it in your face; you're incurably mortal.

This now leads us to a theme that is reiterated throughout the Bible by no one more insistently than by Jesus and Paul. A man must *choose*. He must make up his mind whether he is going to give his heart, his personal attention and (at the practical level) his time, talents and resources, to the things that are temporal, or to the things that are eternal. Where is he going to 'place his money'? Right through the Bible this choice is put before men with the plea that they shall not spend their money on that which is not living bread. There is a type of treasure in which we can invest, which is subject to decay— 'Moth and rust doth corrupt', says Jesus. There is also a heavenly treasure which is indestructible. Sin enters in where men choose to live only for the things that perish.

The Hebrew mind is clearer and more concrete than ours. Rather than speak of comparatives and preferences, the tendency in Hebrew thought is to speak of *loving* this and *hating* that. If God preferred Jacob to Esau, we read that God loved Jacob and hated Esau (Rom 9[13]). If Jesus says that we must put Him before our parents, He brings the whole stark business of choice before our eyes by saying that we must love Him and hate our mother (Lk 14[26]). The lovers of money scoffed at Jesus when He said that a man must either love or hate mammon (Lk 16[13-14]). This may be shocking but it faces facts. So St Paul gives to some the appearance of a Puritan, hating the flesh, despising 'this world's goods'. But he is in fact giving himself and us the old choice—Which matters more to you, this span of seventy years or eternal life? It is better to sit lightly to those things that die, than to be left with a dying soul.

When a Christian becomes fully aware of this choice, he sees it as a matter of urgent decision—in fact, so urgent that he takes up this extreme attitude of 'loving' the things that are eternal, and 'hating' the things that are temporal.

So Charles Wesley cries:

> *No longer we join while sinners invite,*
> *Nor envy the swine their brutish delight;*
> *Their joy is all sadness, their mirth is all vain,*
> *Their laughter is madness, their pleasure is pain.*

'There is a distinction', says Justin, 'between death and death. For this reason the disciples of Christ die daily, torturing their desires and mortifying them according to their divine scriptures; for we have no part at all in shameless desires, and sins impure and glances lewd, or ears attentive to evil, lest our souls thereby be wounded.'[1]

> *O hide this self from me, that I*
> > *No more, but Christ in me, may live!*
> *My vile affections crucify,*
> > *Not let one darling lust survive!*
> *In all things nothing may I see,*
> *Nothing desire or seek, but Thee!*

Let us think of this particularly in relation to our *possessions*. Jesus warns us not to be like the rich fool who has bigger and fuller barns at the expense of an impoverished soul. There is nothing inherently evil about money—but neither is there anything evil about an electric cable charged with 3,000 volts, except that both are dangerous to handle! According to Jesus, it is the possessiveness of possessions which makes it necessary for us to beware of them. It is harder for a rich man to enter the Kingdom of Heaven than for a camel to go through a needle's eye (Mk 10[25]). In fact it is impossible, unless he has the stronger magnet of the grace of God. The care of the world and the deceitfulness of riches choke the word of life (Mt 13[22]). The rich young ruler cannot lay hold on eternal life until he has let go of his possessions (Mk 10[22]). 'Blessed are ye poor', says Jesus, and He means it in the literal as well as in the figurative sense. The life is more than the food, and the body than the raiment (Mt 6[25]). It is almost certain that our Lord Himself died possessing 'nothing but what He stood up in'—a seamless

[1] Justin: *Apology*, xxvi.

robe. And though the foxes of Galilee had holes, the Son of Man had not where to lay His head. The Christian does well to remember that, however much the life of his home may be sacred, there is nothing eternal about the fabric of his house.

> *No foot of land do I possess,*
> *No cottage in this wilderness,*
> *A poor wayfaring man,*
> *I lodge awhile in tents below;*
> *Or gladly wander to and fro,*
> *Till I my Canaan gain.*

Here again St Paul is not to be charged with saying that possessions are in themselves evil. It is our valuation of them that matters, and whether we are their master or they are ours. 'All things are lawful to me', he says, 'but I shall not allow anything to get the mastery over me' (1 Cor 6[12])—certainly not the things that I put into my belly. 'Charge them that are rich in this present world, that they be not high-minded nor have their hope set on the uncertainty of riches . . . but on God who giveth us richly all things to enjoy . . . that they do good, that they be rich in good works . . . laying up in store for themselves a good foundation against the time to come, that they may lay hold on the life which is life indeed.' This is an echo of the saying of Jesus: 'So is he that layeth up treasure for himself, and is not rich toward God' (Lk 12[21]).

All this is something more than a helpful suggestion for successful living. It concerns the life and death of the soul over which God is our final judge. 'The Son of Man', says Jesus, 'shall render unto every man according to his deeds' (Mt 16[27]). 'Each one of us', says Paul, 'shall give an account of himself to God' (Rom 14[12]). By the reckoning of this heavenly accountancy Paul knows that those who 'have nothing' may yet 'possess all things'. The poor in the eyes of the world can make many rich in the eyes of God (2 Cor 6[10]), even as our Lord Jesus Christ 'though he was rich, yet for your sakes became poor, that ye through his poverty might become rich' (2 Cor 8[9]).

Confidence in the flesh is an illusion. 'What things were

gain to me', says Paul, 'these have I counted loss for Christ. Yea, verily, I count all things to be loss for the excellency of the knowledge of Christ Jesus my Lord: for whom I suffered the loss of all things and do count them but dung, that I may gain Christ and be found in Him' (Phil 3⁷⁻⁸). In no other way could Paul hope to know 'the power of His resurrection'.

The implication of this is that a follower of Jesus must journey with Him yet farther. He must be ready to think lightly of *his own physical welfare*. This does not only apply to the times when a man may be tired of his own body. It may be a proper thing to pray for an aged person who is in pain that 'he may be taken'. At such times the body has the appearance of a brutal straight-jacket, and one longs for the prisoner to be released and freed from his bodily chain. Or again, the disillusioned man may be tired of living.

> *I wish that I could go . . .*
> *And leave my flesh discarded lying,*
> *Like luggage of some departed traveller*
> *Gone one knows not wither.*
>
> *Thus I would turn around*
> *And seeing my cast-off body lying like lumber*
> *I would laugh for joy.*

But this is D. H. Lawrence, *In Trouble and Shame*.

Yet the Christian, *even in the prime of life*, when he is full of the joy of living, if he is true to Christ, will be ready to be parted from his own skin. Ever since Christ arrested me in my teens, I have had a deep hero worship for those who love Him more than their own safety. There is a type of devotion to Christ which gathers into itself all heroism and true recklessness. 'Be not afraid', said Jesus, 'of them which kill the body, but are not able to kill the soul' (Mt 10²⁸). That is the sort of person I honour with all my heart, and though I may never achieve it, that is the sort of person I know I ought to be. 'I hold not my life', says Paul, 'of any account as dear unto myself, so that I may accomplish my course, and the ministry which I received from the Lord Jesus, to testify the gospel of the grace of God' (Acts 20²⁴).

This means that those who have the Mind of Christ are 'in a strait betwixt two' (Phil 1²³). Here is the desire to depart and be with Christ in the indestructible realm of Heaven, which may be far better from a selfish point of view. On the other hand, there is the responsibility to remain willingly 'in the flesh', which may be more needful for the sake of Christ, our neighbour, and ourselves. Our Lord Himself said that He was 'straitened' (Luke 12⁵⁰) until His work was accomplished through His death. Yet He shrank from that death until He knew that His hour was come that He should 'depart out of this world unto the Father' (Jn 13¹).

This tension in the life of the Christian is handled in two ways:

(1) Since his body is the temple of the Holy Ghost, it is God's possession, and it is God alone who can decide how long He wishes 'to keep body and soul together'. When the Christian is at his best, he is not tense, but relaxed, and able to say with Richard Baxter:

> *Lord, it belongs not to my care*
> *Whether I die or live.*

However complicated life may become, however fierce the battle between flesh and spirit, it is not for us to decide the hour of our departure, until we are 'taken with a summons'. If our hand or eye offend us, it may be right for us to cut out the offending member, but this does not mean that we must cut off our head! As with Judas, however remorseful a man may be for his deeds, and though he may come to the conclusion 'that in me, that is in my flesh, dwelleth no good thing' (Rom 7¹⁸), he only adds to his own sin by taking his own life.

Furthermore, the Christian accepts the discipline of life in the body, not with passive resignation, but as a positive offering to his Lord. Next to our own will, the most intimate possession that we hold in trust is our body, and both must be offered to God. Did not Jesus, as part of His self-offering to the Father on behalf of mankind, allow His body to be buffeted? Did He not let them smite Him with rods and the palms of their hands? (Mt 26[67]). Shall not His servants, 'as men doomed to death', be ready to be buffeted also? 'I buffet my body', says Paul, 'I get my body under control' (1 Cor 4[11], 1 Cor 9[27]). (He uses the same word as Jesus employs in describing the widow who got the judge down by her continual coming.)

But it is very important to notice that Paul is not putting in a plea for mortification for its own sake; we are not to make an exhibition of self-discipline. Jesus says that we are not to fast in order to be seen of men. There is no virtue in giving one's body to be burned in martyrdom if it is only in self-love. We live daily *unto the Lord* and we die daily *unto the Lord*. Christian discipline is purposeful. St Francis used to call his body 'Brother Ass', which meant that his body needed both discipline and careful attention. Why? Not in order to groom a prize pony for dressage at the Horse Show, but so that St Francis could have a more effective beast of burden for the running of his Master's errands!

Paul would have no use for health and beauty exercises. The buffeting which Paul advocates is of a quite different order. It is not even the athletic health-culture of the Athenian Games, which, after all, were only rewarded by cheers and a laurel crown and a man's sense of pride in his own physical fitness. If I give my body to the gym-instructor, yet have not the love which seeketh not its own, I am nothing. A modern counterpart of this would be the devoted discipline with which a girl is ready to groom herself for modelling. The discipline may be commendable, but after all, the chief end of it is not to glorify God, but to display her own beauty and commend the couturier's dresses.

There is a type of self-discipline which is abortive, because it is not to the glory of God. Some obscure verses in Colossians have been elucidated in the *New English Bible*: 'Why let people dictate to you: "Do not handle this, do not taste that, do not touch the other"—all of them things that must perish as soon as they are used? That is to follow merely human injunctions and teaching. True, it has an air of wisdom, with its forced piety, its self-mortification, and its severity to the body; but it is of no use at all in combating sensuality' (Col 2²⁰⁻³).

Any day now we may see our generation grow disillusioned about self-indulgence. Many have had their bellyful of sensual pleasures. The salutary teaching of psychologists at the beginning of the century was taken thoroughly to heart and acted upon. 'Away with these Victorian inhibitions,' they said. 'Repression is positively dangerous. Man's instincts need free expression.' The half-truth of this message has been taking its toll, and far too many are the slaves of the passions to which they have given free rein. It is quite possible that a reaction may set in. It may take the form of a fashionable movement advocating some form of asceticism. With strip-tease and bingo in the news, this may seem unlikely; but men do go from one false god to another. Asceticism for merely selfish ends, however, is most certainly not the way of Christ.

The reason the body with its appetites and instincts must be brought into subjection is that it may be *a means* to Christ's *end*. Paul is ready to accept even a messenger of Satan to buffet him if it means that the power of Christ is thereby released in the world (2 Cor 12⁷). So long as I live, I must keep the temple of the Holy Ghost in good repair, not for the sake of self-glory, but for the sake of Christ Himself.

(2) The second fact which releases a Christian from tension is that he need not wait for physical death before he starts enjoying eternal life. Writing about the later phases of Paul's life, Dr Dodd says: 'The hope of glory yet to come remains as a background of his thought, but the foreground is more and more occupied by the contemplation of all the riches of divine grace enjoyed here and now by those who are in Christ Jesus.'[1] The Christian knows that it is inevitable that the temple of his body should suffer from fair wear and tear, but he is not anxious about the cubits of his stature. The process of decay

[1] *Apostolic Preaching and Its Development*, p. 149.

will go on, however much he buffets his body to maintain
its health; even if by reason of strength he outlives his three-
score years and ten, his hope of immortality is in the realm of
the spirit, not of the flesh. So any tension he may feel with the
passing of the years is resolved by a constant remembrance
that though 'the outward man is decaying, yet our inward man
is renewed day by day' (2 Cor 4[16]). Though his earthly garment
is rotting on him, yet Christ is growing in him. He is not
obsessed about growing older, because his attention is set upon
'growing up in all things into him which is the head, even
Christ' (Eph 4[15]).

The man in the street does well to taunt us if our only
message is that of being patient till we get to Heaven. The
whole spirit of man cries out here and now for life which is life
indeed. The Christian answer to the anxiety about old age,
which is now so manifest in the world, is that it is possible, in
this world, through Christ, to grow into a condition of life
which is ageless. He that hath the Son, says Jesus, hath the
life. We lay hold on the eternal life which He implants in the
soul. We are *dying*, says Paul, but look! we are *alive* (2 Cor
6[9]). If Christ be in me, it is not only that He is the way so
that I can follow Him; it is not only that He is the truth, so that
I can learn of Him; it is that He is the life, so that I can say with
Paul: For me to live is Christ and to die is gain (Phil 1[21]). The
Angry Young Man in *Look Back in Anger* who says, 'I am
looking for a warm thrilling voice which will cry Hallelujah,
I'm alive!' would do well to find a Christian who can say with
assurance: 'I live, yet not I but Christ liveth in me.'

When Christ dwells within us, we are aware of a power in
our life which is a strength not our own. It is this power of
Christ in us which enables us to say, 'I can do *all* things
in him which strengtheneth me' (Phil 4[13]).

> *Christ be with me, Christ within me,*
> *Christ behind me, Christ before me,*
> *Christ beside me, Christ to win me,*
> *Christ to comfort and restore me.*

Christ beneath me, Christ above me,
Christ in quiet, Christ in danger,
Christ in hearts of all that love me,
Christ in mouth of friend and stranger.

Francis Kilvert was one day visiting his old friend Joseph Duckett. '"How are you Master Duckett?" "Through mercy", said the old man, with an earnest look from his keen, glittering eyes, "through mercy", he repeated, "I'm holden up wonderful. I have been made a wonder to myself".'

Additional Note

IT MAY be useful to add a list of parallel passages for some who wish to follow this theme further for themselves. It must be said most emphatically that this in no sense consists of quotations by Paul from the sayings of Jesus. In many cases there is only a sympathy of idea and what is shown is that Paul is faithful to the mind of Christ rather than that he reiterates His words. This list, which is not exhaustive, has been compiled over some years and it is hoped that the reader may in his own study of the Bible take up the same biblical hobby, and find his own proof for the contention that the mind of Paul is in harmony with the mind of Christ at every essential point.

It is perhaps worth noting that no significant parallels can be traced in the first three chapters of Ephesians or in 1 and 2 Timothy, and Titus. This may not be unconnected with the fact that these are the very passages in Paul's letters about which it is commonly said that their actual phraseology is from the hand of another.

PAUL	JESUS	PAUL	JESUS
Romans		3^{31}	Mt 5^{17-18}
1^{1-2}	Lk 24^{27} / Lk 18^{31}	4^5	Jn 6^{29}
		4^9	Lk 13^{28-9}
1^5	Mk 13^{10} and 13	4^{17}	Jn 5^{21}
1^{15}	Lk 4^{43}	4^{25}	Mt 20^{28}
1^{16}	Mk 8^{38}	5^3	Mt 5^{11} / Lk 21^{19}
2^2	Mt 7^2 / Mk 4^{24}		
		5^8	Jn 3^{16}
2^6	Mt 16^{27}	6^3	Mk 10^{38} / Mt 28^{19}
2^7	Lk 8^{15}		
2^{16}	Mt 6^4 / Lk 8^{17}	6^{16}	Mt 6^{24} / Jn 8^{34}
2^{17}	Jn 5^{45}	7^{1-3}	Mt 5^{31-2}
2^{19-21}	Mt 15^{14} / Mt 23^2	7^{25}	Mk 14^{38}
		8^1	Jn 15^{6-7}
2^{27}	Mt 12^{41}	8^{14-15}	Mk 14^{36}
3^9	Jn 7^{19}	8^{26}	Mt 20^{22}
3^{21}	Jn 5^{46}	8^{27}	Lk 16^{15}

PAUL	JESUS	PAUL	JESUS
Romans—*cont.*		6^{15}	Jn 15^5
$8^{29\text{-}30}$	Jn 17^{22}	6^{16}	Mk 10^8
8^{33}	Lk 18^7	6^{19}	Jn 2^{21}
8^{37}	Jn 16^{33}		⎧ Jn 8^{32}
9^7	Jn $8^{37\text{-}41}$	7^{22}	⎨ 13^{13}
9^{15}	Mt 20^{15}		⎩ 15^{15}
10^9	Mt 10^{32}	7^{23}	Mk 10^{45}
10^{14}	Jn 17^{20}	8^9	Mt 17^{27}
11^8	Mt 13^{15}		⎧ Mt $25^{40\text{-}5}$
11^{25}	Lk 21^{24}	8^{12}	⎨ Mt 18^6
12^5	Jn 15^5	9^9	Lk 10^7
12^{13}	Mk 9^{41}	9^{19}	Mk 10^{44}
12^{14}	⎧ Mt 5^{44}	9^{22}	Mt 3^{15}
	⎩ Lk 6^{28}	10^{13}	Mt 6^{13}
12^{17}	Mt 5^{39}	10^{16}	Mt $26^{26\text{-}7}$
12^{18} ⎫		10^{21}	Mt 6^{24}
14^{19} ⎬	Mk 9^{50}	10^{32}	Mt 17^{27}
12^{19}	Mt 5^{39}	11^1	Jn 13^{15}
13^1	Jn 19^{11}		⎧ Mt $26^{26\text{-}8}$
13^7	⎧ Mt 17^{24}	11^{23}	⎨ Mk $14^{22\text{-}4}$
	⎩ Mt 22^{21}		⎩ Lk $22^{17\text{-}19}$
$13^{8\text{-}9}$	Mt 22^{39}	11^{31}	Mt 7^1
13^{11}	Lk 21^{28}	12^{13}	Jn $7^{38\text{-}9}$
13^{12}	Jn 9^4	13^1	⎧ Mt 7^{21}
13^{13}	Lk 21^{34}		⎩ Jn 15^{12}
$14^{10\text{-}13}$	⎧ Mt $7^{1\text{-}3}$	13^2	Mt 17^{20}
	⎩ Mt 12^{36}	14^{20}	Mt 10^{16}
14^{14}	⎧ Mk 7^{15}	15^3	⎧ Mk 10^{45}
	⎩ Mt 15^{19}		⎩ Lk $24^{25\text{-}6}$
	⎧ Jn 5^{30}	15^{10}	Mt 10^{20}
15^3	⎨ Jn 6^{38}	$15^{27\text{-}28}$	Mt 11^{27}
	⎩ Lk 22^{42}	15^{31}	Lk $9^{23\text{-}4}$
15^8	⎧ Mt 15^{24}	15^{36}	Jn 12^{24}
	⎩ Mt 10^5	15^{50}	Mt 16^{17}
16^{19}	Mt 10^{16}	15^{57}	Jn 16^{33}
16^{20}	Lk 10^{17}		
		2 Corinthians	
		1^{18}	Mt 5^{37}
1 Corinthians		2^3	Jn 15^{11}
1^{13}	Mt 28^{19}	4^4	Jn 9^{39}
1^{17}	Jn 4^2	4^{11}	Lk $9^{23\text{-}4}$
1^{22}	⎧ Mk 8^{11}	5^1	⎧ Lk 16^9
	⎩ Mt 12^{38}		⎩ Jn 14^2
1^{27}	Mt 11^{25}	5^{10}	Mt $25^{31\text{-}2}$
2^{10}	Mt 13^{11}	5^{21}	Mk 15^{34}
2^{16}	Jn 15^{15}	8^9	Jn 17^5
3^{11}	Mt 7^{24}	10^1	Mt 11^{25}
3^{18}	Mt 11^{25}	12^{13}	Mt $10^{9\text{-}10}$
6^1	Mt $18^{15\text{-}17}$	13^3	Mt 10^{20}
6^7	Mt 5^{39}		

PAUL	JESUS	PAUL	JESUS
Galatians		4^3	Lk 10^{20}
1^{10}	Mt 6^{24}	4^6	Mt $6^{25\text{-}32}$
1^{24}	Mt 5^{16}		
3^7	Mt 8^{11}	Colossians	
4^{14}	{ Mt 10^{40} Mk 9^{37} Lk 10^{16} Jn 13^{20}	1^9	Lk $22^{31\text{-}2}$
		1^{17}	Jn 8^{58}
		1^{19}	Jn 17^{21}
		$3^{13\text{-}14}$	{ Lk 6^{36} Jn 15^{12}
5^{14}	Mt 22^{39}	3^{15}	Jn 14^{27}
6^1	Mt 18^{15}	3^{16}	{ Jn 15^3 $17^{8\text{-}17}$
Ephesians		3^{23}	Mt 25^{40}
4^{32}	{ Mt 6^{12} Jn 13^{34}	3^{24}	Mt 16^{27}
5^1	Mt 5^{48}	4^6	Mt 5^{13}
5^4	Mt 12^{36}		
5^8	Mt 5^{14}	1 Thessalonians	
5^{12}	Jn 3^9	1^4	Jn 15^{16}
5^{13}	Mt 10^{26}	1^6	Jn 16^{33}
5^{21}	Jn 13^{14}	2^{15}	Mt 23^{31}
5^{31}	{ Mt 19^5 Mk 10^8	4^9	Jn 6^{45}
6^{12}	Lk 22^{53}	4^{15}	Mt 16^{28}
		4^{16}	Mt 26^{28}
Philippians		$5^{2\text{-}6}$	Mt $24^{42\text{-}3}$
1^{11}	Jn 15^2	5^{13}	{ Jn 14^{11} Mk 9^{50}
1^{12}	Lk $21^{12\text{-}13}$	5^{16}	Lk 11^8
1^{21}	Mt 10^{28}		
2^3	Mk $10^{43\text{-}4}$	2 Thessalonians	
2^5	Mt 20^{28}	1^5 and ^{11}	{ Lk 20^{35} Mt 22^8
2^7	Jn 13^{14}	2^3	Mt 24^6
2^8	Mt 26^{42}	2^9	Mt 24^{24}
2^9	Mt 26^{64}	2^{13}	Jn 15^{16}
2^{10}	Mt 28^{18}	3^3	Jn 17^{15}
2^{15}	Jn 8^{12}	3^6	Mt 18^{17}
2^{16}	Lk 6^{23}	3^{15}	Mt 18^{15}
3^2	Mt 7^{15}		
3^8	Mt $6^{25\text{-}6}$